GAG-ORDERED NO MORE

THE 800-POUND GORILLA IN THE U.S. GOVERNMENT

Praise for Gag-Ordered No More...

Rather than being gagged by political appointees and hamstrung by bureaucrats, Brian Czech should have been treated as a hero for raising awareness of the conflict between economic growth and environmental protection. One thing is for sure: Czech's civil service legacy will be more durable than that of his suppressors.

Doug La Follette, five-time Wisconsin Secretary of State

Brian Czech is perhaps the world's most tireless and effective advocate for a steady state economy. This did not serve him well in his career with the U.S. Fish and Wildlife Service, where any talk of the conflict between growth and conservation was squashed. Written in a folksy, easy-to-read style that also manages to convey justified outrage over our continued destruction of the planet, *Gag-Ordered No More* offers insightful analysis of the existential ecological crises we face. We can only hope that the FWS follows Czech's advice for reform, but we can be certain that—gag-ordered no more—Czech will be an even more powerful voice for economic sanity and a steady state economy.

Joshua Farley, past president, International Society for Ecological Economics

Books like *Gag-Ordered No More* are crucial to remind us of the importance of civil servants swearing allegiance to the rule of law and the Constitution and not to any political party, ideology, or individual. What people like Brian Czech experience in exposing the truth in government is unfortunately a byproduct of leadership, or rather lack of leadership. It is a fear among so-called leaders that their mistakes will cast a dark shadow on their careers rather than a recognition that mistakes are simply part of civil service and nothing to be afraid of. Mistakes are learning opportunities, and those who expose mistakes—like Czech did—pave the way for improvement. Ultimately, is that not what we need from our civil servants?

Richard Ceballos, Deputy District Attorney, Los Angeles

In a world where seemingly anyone can say anything, Brian Czech's experience of being systematically gagged by the U.S. government is stunning. With characteristic candor and spirit, Czech vividly describes the unthinkable lengths a federal agency went, over decades and through multiple administrations, to prevent him from speaking about the conflict between economic growth and ecological integrity. This was not just a case of speaking truth to power, but of speaking truth, period. Shocking in its eye-popping details of the inner workings of a federal agency, the story of Czech's determined struggle to speak openly and honestly about the perils of relentless economic growth as a public policy goal is deeply informative, uplifting, and perhaps a dare for each of us to do the same.

Vera Cole, past president, Mid-Atlantic Renewable Energy Association

Brian Czech was the rare civil servant who understood the conflict between economic growth and environmental protection, in spades. Such an understanding leads to hard questions for an agency whose mission is wildlife conservation. Why are we doing this, why aren't we doing that, and why are we ignoring the challenge of economic growth? These questions make political appointees and ladder-climbing bureaucrats uncomfortable; the response is simply to halt the questioning. In this incredibly well-written account of agency censorship, Czech gets the last word, helping to inspire the civil servants of today and tomorrow to tell the truth about the conflict between growth and conservation.

Bill Wilen, retired Chief, National Wetlands Inventory, U.S. Fish and Wildlife Service

As another former federal employee who entered civil service in hopes of working for the 'common good,' I can corroborate Czech's realization that the Senior Executive Service makes sure that the bureaucracy serves only politically powerful (meaning mostly 'monied') interests. Americans can't depend on the federal government to necessarily do the right thing. Dr. Czech was extremely brave for doggedly trying to pull an incredibly important but inconvenient truth up the civil service ladder. Thank you for telling your story.

Robert Fireovid, former National Program Leader, Agricultural Research Service, U.S. Department of Agriculture

Free speech can be very costly, especially if you speak the truth in a world that prefers illusions. Brian Czech paid a high price repeatedly for insisting that the U.S. Fish and Wildlife Service—the agency he worked tirelessly for—do its part to raise public awareness of the conflict between economic growth and biodiversity conservation. His reward was a personnel file replete with gag orders, reprimands, and suspensions. Now that he's 'out' and the gag removed, his clarion call rings free at last.

William Rees, Professor Emeritus, University of British Columbia

Truth-tellers are a commodity in short supply today. Brian Czech is a truth-teller. Over a long career, Czech has argued unflinchingly that the pursuit of eternal economic growth is unsustainable—by definition—and at odds with the health of our planet. In *Gag-Ordered No More*, Czech details the personal ordeals and sacrifices he endured within the bureaucracy of the U.S. Fish and Wildlife Service for simply telling the truth that conserving biodiversity is incompatible with economic growth. His story is not only a compelling read; it also serves as an inspiration for all of us to stand up, do the right thing, and tell the unvarnished truth.

John Mirisch, three-time mayor of Beverly Hills, California

Gag-Ordered No More describes how and why the leadership of the U.S. Fish and Wildlife Service suppressed the truth about economic growth, abused their authority, and destroyed agency morale. Thankfully it also presents bold ideas for how the agency could serve a public that expects it to be a model for ecosystem protection.

Russell England, retired fisheries biologist and author of Gross Deceptive Product

I highly recommend this book to those who want to understand why we continue to say we love the Earth and want to protect it, yet continue to destroy it with our incessant push for economic growth.

Kent Shifferd, author of The Planetary Emergency

Brian Czech brought to the U.S. Fish and Wildlife Service an impressive background in conservation biology and ecological economics, with a specialty on the conflict between economic growth and wildlife conservation. While supported by professional peers, senior management did their utmost to squash his efforts with reprimands, gag orders and various forms of harassment. One of the remarkable aspects of Czech's tale is how tenaciously he persisted despite the restrictions placed on him. At the same time, he wisely established an NGO to focus on this critically important issue that is ignored by so many, and formed the Center for the Advancement of the Steady State Economy. My foundation provided some of the seed funding for CASSE and it was one of the best investments we ever made.

Jack Santa Barbara, Ph.D., retired CEO and Director of the Santa Barbara Family Foundation

GAG-ORDERED NO MORE

THE 800-POUND GORILLA IN THE U.S. GOVERNMENT

BRIAN CZECH

STEADY STATE PRESS
ARLINGTON, VA

Copyright © 2023 Brian Czech

All rights reserved. No part of this book may be reproduced in any form or by any electronic or mechanical means, including information storage or retrieval systems, without permission in writing from the publisher, except by reviewers, who may quote brief passages in a review.

ISBN: 978-1-7329933-7-2

Edited by Gary Gardner
Book design by Gary Gardner

Cover design by Elisabeth Heissler

Printed and bound in USA
First printing November 2023

Published by Steady State Press (an imprint of CASSE, the Center for the Advancement of the Steady State Economy)
1100 N. Glebe Road
Suite 1010
Arlington, VA USA 22201

www.steadystate.org

Dedicated to Richard Ceballos,

Deputy District Attorney, Los Angeles,

who chose the challenging path of truth

in the face of

*bureaucratic mediocrity, political pressure, and
moral turpitude.*

CONTENTS

Acknowledgments	xii
Foreword	xiii
Preface: They Wanted Me Out; Now I'm Out	xv

PART ONE   Introducing the 800-Pound Gorilla   1
1. Pontius Pilate Comes to Tucson — 3
2. The Perfect Job — 7
3. A Tale of Two Briefings — 17
4. Non-Privy Presidents — 29
5. Ecological Integrity vs. the 800-Pound Gorilla — 37

PART TWO   Under Damocles' Sword   49
6. The Bible Club and Gag-Order Creep — 51
7. The "Bold Ideas Forum" Gets Scrubbed from the Internet — 59
8. Reprimands, Suspensions, and a Rigged Appeals Process — 75
9. Babies in the Bathwater of the 800-Pound Gorilla — 85

PART THREE   Reforming the U.S. Fish and Wildlife Service   99
10. Joy-Riding on Taxpayer Dollars: A Refuge System Travelogue — 101
11. "Dumbing it Down" is Conducive to Dummies — 115
12. True Conservation: A Vision Worthy of a Director — 121

Epilogue	131
Bibliography	135
Index	141

ACKNOWLEDGMENTS

I extend my sincere gratitude to Linda Andraesen, Paul Angermeier, David Blockstein, Jim and Eldeen Carpenter, Steve Coghlan, Vera Cole, Rick Coleman, Scott Covington, Rob Dietz, Penny Firth, Jimmy Fox, Rob Harding, Bob Hughes, Susan Jewell, Mike Larson, Greg Mikkelson, Phil Pister, Heather Reynolds, Bill Rees, Steve Sheffield, Cole Thompson, David Trauger, and Bill Wilen for their support during various phases of my government career.

Gary Gardner, Kathy Granillo, and Jason Leppig provided expert opinions and editorial advice. Not all advice was taken, but all was appreciated. Nothing in this book implies their agreement or disagreement with the facts and opinions herein.

The Steady State Press owes its existence to donors such as Peter Seidel, Jack Santa-Barbara, Tom Crain, Greg Newswanger, John and Deborah Rohe, and other like-minded citizens who favor an honest and open approach to sustainability and public policy.

I have long appreciated the efforts and results of Public Employees for Environmental Responsibility, including staff and leaders who helped me at various stages of my struggle to speak truth to power. Tim Whitehouse, Jeff Ruch, and Kirsten Stade come most readily to mind.

I fondly memorialize the late Herman Daly, my mentor in steady-state economics; E.O. Wilson, a late-comer but strong convert to steady-state economics; and Lisa Vandemark, a brilliant sounding board who left us far too early.

I reserve special gratitude for Sukanya Venkataraman, who bore the brunt of the negative vibes inevitably emanating from a chronically gagged civil servant.

FOREWORD

Easy to read, insightful, and thought-provoking, *Gag-Ordered No More* is a first-person account of Brian Czech's struggle to introduce the concepts of conservation biology and ecological economics to his work at the U.S. Fish and Wildlife Service. His efforts were met with outright hostility by managers in the Service intent on preserving the status quo. Challenging the status quo in a government agency is never an easy thing. It takes courage and perseverance; Czech is tenacious and knows this is a fight worth having.

Czech has a Ph.D. in renewable natural resources studies and has focused the latter half of his career on the relationship between economic growth and biodiversity conservation. He was hired in 1999 as among the first conservation biologists in the Fish and Wildlife Service. Working at National Wildlife Refuge System headquarters, he sought to bring an interdisciplinary approach, including an expertise in ecological economics.

Czech's struggles in this effort are worthy of a Kurt Vonnegut novel. My favorite is when managers skittish with the concept of "ecological integrity" replaced the ecological integrity policy with the "23-syllable, non-flowing, bureaucratically bumbling 'Biological Integrity, Diversity, and Environmental Health Policy.'"

But beneath the frolicking read found in many parts of this book, Czech keeps us focused on the critical issues at stake—"the planetary ecosystem may be irrevocably unraveling toward a new, devastating reality." While not apparent to many, we are in the midst of a great extinction. And unlike previous extinction events, this mass extinction is driven by humankind's unsustainable use of land, water, and natural resources.

However, to many in the federal government and in halls of major think tanks and environmental organizations, discussing the links between species loss and economic growth is a non-starter, and those who raise the topic do so at their own professional peril.

Czech lived this reality for many years. When he began to raise awareness of the trade-off between economic growth and wildlife conservation, Refuge System leadership got cold feet and started issuing gag orders. As a scientist passionate about conservation, Czech refused to ignore the "800-Pound Gorilla" and was subjected to reprimands, suspensions, and a general abuse of authority.

Raising issues associated with economic growth has been a non-starter for a long time in Washington. Everybody with power wants to discuss the win-win: We can have all the growth we want and not sacrifice our natural world. After all, economic growth has provided those of us with power a lifestyle unparalleled in human history. For managers in the National Wildlife Refuge System, it meant good pay, great per diems to travel to many interesting places, and the camaraderie one finds in the after-hours drinking club, aptly called the Bible Club.

As Czech found out, upsetting the applecart can be professionally treacherous and hazardous to the health of civil servants.

To go through what Czech went through, you have to be tough. Czech's toughness probably comes from a background few in the federal government can match. Before getting his Ph.D., he was a meat packer, ranch hand, construction worker, firefighter, wilderness ranger, thinning crew foreman, wildlife technician, and wildlife biologist. He'd "worked in eight states and had developed the wildlife management program on the fourth largest Indian reservation in the country, the San Carlos Apache Reservation in Arizona."

So why did Czech move to the political jungle of the Washington, DC beltway and persist with his efforts to raise awareness of the 800-Pound Gorilla? Why didn't he sit back and accept the gag orders and live the comfortable life of many government employees?

Czech shares his story in a compelling, thoughtful, and meaningful way. His struggle is inherently a David-versus-Goliath struggle. The Department of the Interior, which the Fish and Wildlife Service is part of, holds all the cards. Czech faced what many dissenters face: an organization that creates a hostile workplace and socially ostracizes and isolates those who think outside the box.

At one point in his writing, Czech calls the book a downer, and in some parts, it is. But overall, he carefully weaves a story that offers hope and redemption and provides recommendations for improving government service. It is an important read for anyone interested in thinking about how we can be better stewards of the earth and who wants to understand better what we must do to make government service honorable.

Plus, I found it compelling because I do not doubt that Brian Czech is on the right side of history.

Tim Whitehouse, J.D.
Executive Director
Public Employees for Environmental Responsibility (PEER)

PREFACE

THEY WANTED ME OUT; NOW I'M OUT

They say the ironies never cease. Did you know that freedom of speech, that cornerstone of the American Constitution, is practically irrelevant in the American government? Prisoners, illegal aliens, and racists have freedom of speech pursuant to the First Amendment. Civil servants? Not so much, which is doubly ironic because: 1) the First Amendment originally applied *only* to the federal government, and 2) the First Amendment is enforced *by* the federal government.

Of course, some speech can be treacherous enough to be unconstitutional, no matter who you are. You're not allowed to yell "fire" in a crowded theatre, at least not as a prank. And even most prisoners, undocumented immigrants, and yes, lowly federal employees would question the right to hate speech, certain heavy-metal lyrics, and treasonous rhetoric.

But we're not talking here about any of the obvious scenarios in which free speech may be illegal or odious. What Americans need to know is that, if you're a federal employee and the boss doesn't want you saying, for example, "clean coal is an oxymoron," you won't be saying it for long. Not on the job, at least, where the vast majority of your professional expertise should be used. And maybe not elsewhere, either, depending on the length of the agency's tentacles.

What this means is that taxpayers cannot expect their civil servants to tell them the truth, especially the whole truth. On some topics, federal employees can't even tell *each other* the truth! You could be the foremost expert on a topic of grave concern to humanity, but if you're a federal employee and the boss is more concerned about climbing the ladder than delivering the truth, humanity be damned.

If you didn't know the First Amendment was sawed off for federal employees, you're certainly not alone. In fact, most federal employees don't even know. Oddly enough, the most experienced ones are the least likely to know. How could that be? Because the First Amendment worked fine in the halls of government until 2006, when the U.S. Supreme Court decided it shouldn't. Some of the older bureaucrats never got the memo—this is probably the first they've heard of it—whereas younger bureaucrats were practically born into this brave new world.

The case was *Garcetti v. Ceballos*, whereby five Supreme Court justices choked most of the life out of government employees' freedom of speech. The other four stuck with a less cynical vision of our constitutional democracy, asserting that the First Amendment applies fully to everyone in the United States, with exceptions pertaining to the *type* of speech, not to who is speaking.[1] They must have felt strongly about it, too, and for more reasons than one. *Garcetti* was one of those rare cases for which three separate dissents were written; namely, by Justices Stevens, Souter, and Breyer. (Justice Ginsburg joined Souter's dissent.)

I didn't know my First Amendment right to freedom of speech had been terminated on the job at U.S. Fish and Wildlife Service headquarters until I started getting the gag orders. But once the gag orders started turning into reprimands and suspensions, I *really* knew.

But I'm no longer a federal employee—my "tour of duty" is in the rearview mirror—and now I'm going to help Americans discover why and how the political appointees running our government agencies suppress the truth, abuse their authority, destroy agency morale, and forsake the taxpayer in more ways than one. All with the blessing of the Supreme Court—albeit a heavily contested, slimmest possible majority thereof.

The truths revealed herein will likely be shocking to many. Government suppression of speech takes the form of a never-ending soap opera, and with real-life, disastrous consequences. We've all heard the jingle attributed to Sir Walter Scott, circa 1800, "Oh what a tangled web we weave, when first we practice to deceive." Herein I'll duly report on a 21st century tangled web of bureaucratic deceit, woven by political appointees, bought and paid for by the American public.

If you think these topics will be troubling for *you*, don't feel too bad. It could be worse: You could be *me*. The act of writing this book was an exceptional downer for yours truly, the recipient of the political suppression in question and the subject of a long-running series of bureaucratic beatings. For me, this was no mere analysis of subject matter, but a psychological plunge back into an icy pool of disrespect, humility, and frustration.

In case the phrase "gag order" is unclear, it is simply a directive, a demand, an order per se to cease and desist from all communications pertaining to a particular topic. The phrase is used most often in the context of legal

---

[1] For example, obscenity, child pornography, and "true threats" are not protected speech. (See Ruane 2014.)

proceedings, when the parties to a lawsuit—as well as their attorneys—are gagged by court order.

Probably the next most common use of the phrase is in the government, at least since *Garcetti v. Ceballos*. The political appointee or bureaucrat who issues a gag order will euphemistically call it a "memorandum of expectations." When I received my first one, I confided in a higher-level official about the implications of this shocking memo. Once I described the memo, he immediately replied, "Oh, you got a gag order?!"

After my fourth one, it occurred to me that everyone in government should have to experience a gag order for a month or two, in order to develop an understanding of the psychological impact and sociological effects in the workplace. While at first a gag order can be simply frustrating, it has the potential to become depressing, torturous, and even ruinous. A gag order can become like a cancer, metastasizing into the employee's body of work, crippling the employee's career, taking a toll on personal life, and ultimately harming the agency as well. The political appointee or bureaucratic chief who would gag a hardworking civil servant should have a taste of the medicine before prescribing such a sickening "cure."

Of course, not all gag orders are created equal. What if a tax-paid—and extremely *well*-paid—employee droned ad nauseum about his first car, or maybe his high school football-playing days, accomplishing nothing in the process and wasting the time of captive co-workers? Presumably the employee could cease and desist, in order to continue drawing a handsome salary and benefits. Even then, though, the issuance of a formal gag order would hardly be necessary. Assuming capable leadership was available, the employee would get the message that, "You're boring people and wasting our time."

Now, however, imagine you spent five years of Ph.D. research and post-doctoral studies on a topic that virtually everyone—even the ones doing the gagging—agreed was essential to the mission of your agency and critical to the nation's environmental and economic wellbeing. That's five years of time, money, and intensive effort and determination.

Imagine, further, that your expertise on the topic was one of the reasons you were hired by the agency to begin with. Imagine that leadership in the agency was originally supportive of advancing the topic to the broader agency, policymakers, and the public.

Imagine, too, that you'd been invited to speak on the topic at dozens of universities around the world. You'd given keynote addresses at numerous scientific, professional conferences, and you'd addressed the General Assembly of the United Nations. You'd spoken about the topic with Cabinet-level officials, economic advisors to the President, and a dozen or so diplomats. You'd often been encouraged and even exhorted by these higher officials to keep the discussion going, due to the crucial nature of the topic.

Then, imagine that the leadership in your agency—a tiny corner of the world—was replaced practically overnight by a bureaucratically inbred chain of command that collectively acted like a bull in a china shop. Imagine this chain of command treating the agency like its oyster for personal enjoyment, running roughshod over previous programs and priorities. Finally, imagine getting a gag order pertaining to your hard-earned, expensive expertise.

Now *that's* the type of gag order everyone in government should experience, especially the political appointees and the various "chiefs" in position to short-circuit the First Amendment.

Based on what you've read thus far, you may get the impression that this civil servant, at least, wasn't easily gagged. And you're right. Every change of supervisor, every relevant issue that arose, even the slow passage of time… always there were reasons to test the waters with the "800-Pound Gorilla" (to be revealed in Chapter 1). My reluctance to abide by the gag orders—along with ham-handed agency leadership—explains the frequency, number, and severity of the gag orders I accumulated. It literally got to the point where I was hardly allowed to talk about *anything*, with *anyone*![2]

Career in shambles, I was put on such a short leash that the chafing of my neck became nearly unbearable. By then, in early 2016, I was seldom seen smiling in the hallways, especially with chiefs around.

As if that wasn't enough to make me *want* to retire, I was informed in indirect yet perfectly clear terms that I *should* retire, or at least resign from the agency. I had sunk 20 years—over a third of my life—into federal service, with a passionate interest in raising awareness of the 800-Pound Gorilla. Furthermore, I was only a few years away from retirement eligibility with full federal benefits. And now, career in tatters, workplace relations spoiled, and surrounded by ladder-climbing supervisors, it looked like I was going to have to call it quits.

---

[2] The last chief I worked for prohibited me from talking with *anyone* about *anything* without first seeking his permission. No talking in the halls, no phone calls, no dropping by the office of a colleague to say hello. This was not a written order—it was impossible for the chief to enforce and wouldn't withstand legal scrutiny—but it was communicated in no uncertain terms. It was finally rescinded after about six months, when I threatened to file a harassment claim. Meanwhile it remained a constant source of tension, dysfunction, and frustration.

But I didn't. I performed every demeaning task slathered onto my plate. During my final two years of federal service, I did secretarial work, edited briefing statements, and handled various logistics. Not that I did so cheerfully. I'd been harassed, hamstrung, and humiliated. I'd had my job title changed and my duties downgraded. I'd been moved to a stuffy little office without windows, and then to a cubicle. I'd been taken off teams and prevented from networking with other agencies. My name disappeared from contact lists and I'd been removed from any consideration of advancement. And, although I wasn't in it for the money, I'd lost hundreds of thousands of dollars in salary that, in a reasonably progressive environment with career advancement based upon merit, would have accrued by then.

But I didn't quit. I kept my mouth shut and my head down and I did the job, biding my time.

One veteran co-worker who knew some of the story said simply, "I don't know how you do it," and I'm sure a few others wondered the same. Yet most staff had no idea what was happening, and such is the essence of gag ordering. I and the 800-Pound Gorilla had become an afterthought to agency leadership. Head down and taciturn, I was a closed book to young staffers and an unknown to recent political appointees. The gag orders had worked, at least in the short term.

In the final stage of my career, the only ones paying any attention to me were lower-level branch chiefs who, collectively, were like the sadistic prison warden from *Shawshank Redemption*. To clarify, they probably weren't as sadistic as the warden, but they were every bit as arrogant. They knew nothing about the 800-Pound Gorilla, but they knew about the long-running gag order, and they enforced it ruthlessly. And like the Shawshank prisoner, I worked hard, acted civilly, and produced results while I strategized about options.

Toward the end of President Obama's second term in the White House, I was "set free" for a six-month detail with a different agency, where I was put in charge of a broad initiative and had, once again, the ability to network and collaborate. My new colleagues and I quickly developed a camaraderie I hadn't experienced in decades. Most importantly, leadership in the host agency treated me fairly and with respect. I looked forward to each new day in the office, and I invoked creative powers that hadn't been tapped in years. My performance was rated "outstanding."

The ironies were mounting and the possibility of a rejuvenated federal career was almost palpable. But alas, it was too late, especially when my home agency pulled me back into their headquarters in the early months of the Trump Administration. By then I wasn't interested in starting over with FWS. Too much damage had been done. The baggage was too heavy, the hurdles too high, and I'd long lost respect for agency "leadership." Some of the lower chiefs had finally figured out I wasn't the enemy after all, but the higher chiefs and political appointees had shown their stripes one too many times.

Frankly, by then I had a new plan. I meted out my energies carefully, performing my twisted day job while writing an exposé at lunchtimes, nights, and weekends. Sometimes I even wrote my lunchtime entries in the café of Fish and Wildlife headquarters.

The exposé got longer and longer until finally it looked like a book, warranting a preface.

They wanted me out, and now I'm out. As for the 800-Pound Gorilla? Well, let's put it this way: *Gag-Ordered No More!*

Part One

INTRODUCING THE 800-POUND GORILLA

Three things cannot be long hidden: the sun, the moon, and the truth.

The Buddha

1

PONTIUS PILATE COMES TO TUCSON

Jesus Christ, nailed to the cross and suspended with exceptionally long wires, hovered above the thousand or so citizens assembled in Tucson, making peace in an atmosphere of latent heat. Such a setting—smack dab in St. Mark's United Methodist Church—was the brainchild of the Kolbe camp. Congressman Jim Kolbe, a Republican from Arizona, was a mollifier best known for being little known for over a decade, until coming out as gay in 1996.

Personally, I couldn't have cared if Kolbe was gay, straight, or halfway inclined to deviate. But Kolbe made a big deal of announcing his gayness because he had just voted in favor of the Defense of Marriage Act, which was *against* gay marriage. Naturally his vote infuriated the gay and lesbian community. So Kolbe came out of the closet to hold on to as much of the gay and lesbian vote as possible, in order to retain the status and privilege of "Member, United States House of Representatives."

Now *that's* a politician!

After a year or two things died down for Kolbe, and arguably the remaining highlight of his career was being replaced in Congress by the principled Gabby Giffords in 2006. Meanwhile he tried to keep a low profile and largely succeeded. He had maneuvered his way into a cushy job with tons of perks and didn't like to make waves.

With such a propensity to mollify and assuage, Kolbe would have made an even better political appointee than politician per se. Unlike the professional politician, the appointee doesn't even have to get re-elected. The appointee, if willing to bend like an eel in the tides, can often survive a change in elected leadership without the cost, hassle, or stress of campaigning.

So it was no surprise that, for the public hearing at St. Mark's, Kolbe called in the political appointees, senior executives, and select high-level bureaucrats for bending in the necessary directions and serving up the opiates to the masses. This, he felt, was needed because the good citizens of Tucson were fomenting opposition to the federal government, namely, the U.S. Fish and Wildlife Service (FWS), which had proposed to designate a local area as "critical habitat" for a species known as the "cactus ferruginous pygmy owl."

It was January 7, 1998, and Kolbe knew that endangered species could bring political tidal waves, especially in those years when the northern spotted owl had proved so divisive in the Pacific Northwest. Along with critters like the red-cockaded woodpecker in the Southeast, prairie dog in the Great Plains, and desert tortoise in the Southwest, the cactus ferruginous pygmy owl was a relatively unheralded species that nevertheless had the official status to foil the best-laid plans of landowners, developers, local governments, regional authorities, and even federal agencies. Each of these species, and hundreds more, had been listed as threatened or endangered pursuant to the Endangered Species Act of 1973, affording them protections from pipelines, power plants, and other projects capable of significant habitat destruction.

In the case of the pygmy owl, the immediate concern of the Tucson citizenry was the construction of a high school. Designating critical habitat for the owl would have prevented construction in the preferred location of the Amphitheatre School District in northwest Tucson. Therefore the pygmy owl had the potential to evoke emotions exceeding those arising from purely economic concerns. How dare the federal government even think of prioritizing some bird—a pygmy version no less—above the kids' education!

On the other hand, as a cultural capital of the Desert Southwest, Tucson has plenty of citizens concerned about conservation. Tucson proudly boasts the University of Arizona, well-known for its five-star evolution and ecology departments, a highly reputable School of Renewable Natural Resources, and the environmentally focused Udall Center for Studies in Public Policy. Numerous county, state, and federal offices centered on conservation issues dot the city and county maps. Environmental consulting firms do brisk business with the university, government agencies, and the business community. The Sonoran Desert Museum, Saguaro National Monument, and Reid Park Zoo help maintain citizen awareness of conservation issues, particularly the plight of endangered species. To top it all off, the region around Tucson is naturally blessed with high levels of biological diversity and endemism (meaning that numerous species are found there and nowhere else). Due to the combination of these circumstances, the Tucson polity has frequent and nuanced conversations about species conservation.

Therefore it was an insult to the intelligence of taxpayers young and old, university students and scholars, businessmen and civil servants alike, when the Washington, DC representative of the U.S. Fish and Wildlife Service strode up to the podium and cynically announced, right there under the crucifix, "We all know that there is no conflict between growing the economy and protecting endangered species." It was as if the spirit of Pontius Pilate had invaded the sanctimonious setting. Here was a fellow willing to wash his hands of the truth, as long as it kept the crowd from getting too rambunctious—and more importantly, as long as it kept him in good standing with his political overseers.

For me in particular, this political appointee's pronouncement sounded like fingernails on a chalkboard.[3] I knew he was way off base because I was a hard-core student and scholar of the subject matter at hand. My Ph.D. program—almost completed at the time—was focused precisely on the relationship between economic growth and biodiversity conservation.

Not that my dissertation was titled, "The Relationship between Economic Growth and Biodiversity Conservation." It probably could have been, but my research covered more ground than that and the title was actually, "The Endangered Species Act, American Democracy, and an Omnibus Role for Public Policy." I had analyzed the Endangered Species Act with a fine-toothed comb, using a model called "policy design theory." Policy design theory entails a wide-ranging analysis of the policy in question plus the context in which the policy must operate.

One of the methods I used to analyze the context of the Endangered Species Act was to account for the *reasons* that 877 (at the time) species had been listed by FWS as threatened or endangered. What was causing their demise? Was there a common theme among all these listings?

Yes, there was. I published a summary of it in *Science* and a more thorough assessment in *Bioscience*.[4] For our purposes, suffice it to say that the causes of species decline in the United States were simply a who's who of the American economy: agriculture, mining, logging, manufacturing, urbanization, etc. So there we have our 800-Pound Gorilla: It's the economy or, more specifically, economic growth.

Whether you're pro-growth or not, you should at least be aware of the

---

[3] At the time, the person in question was probably classified as a "senior executive." However, many if not most senior executives would be considered political appointees for most purposes. They are often selected to the Senior Executive Service for very political reasons; they are political appointees in effect.

[4] See Czech and Krausman 1997 and Czech et al. 2000, respectively.

trade-offs associated with growth. In fact, you can't really say with any credibility that you are pro-growth, anti-growth, or even neutral on the topic unless you understand the consequences—positive and negative—*of* growth.

During the open forum in Tucson, I stood up and objected to the appointee's rhetoric that "there is no conflict between growing the economy and protecting endangered species." I gave a thirty-second summation of my research, including the who's who of species endangerment. Rather than merely highlighting the problem of economic growth, I noted a solution as well, namely, a non-growing, non-declining economy. This "steady state economy" would slow the fast-flowing stream of new threats to species and was the key to long-run biodiversity conservation.

The front man from FWS kept a pleasant demeanor as he gave a perfectly ambiguous response. It was obvious that the concepts were new to the fellow, and at least he didn't try to refute my findings. Not knowing him, and knowing little about how FWS operated, I had no idea whether there was any hope for him to reform his rhetoric, so I sought him out afterward. He actually congratulated me for a good job of articulating an important point and promised to consider the matter going forward.

He did, but with a cynical political calculus and, ultimately, a propensity to gag-order.

2

THE PERFECT JOB

We might surmise that ideas—and ideals—flourish at colleges and universities. That's common sense. The more time one spends on a college campus, the more developed the ideas and ideals become. It doesn't take a Ph.D. to understand the math.

It does, however, take approximately 24 years of school to get a Ph.D. That doesn't mean it has to be a straight 24 years in an ivory tower, disconnecting the student from reality.

In my case, the years at the Universities of Wisconsin, Washington, and Arizona were interspersed with even more years of work. Starting no later than junior high school I almost always had a job. By the time my Ph.D. research started at the University of Arizona, I had been a meat packer (a "Green Bay packer" no less), ranch hand, construction worker, firefighter, wilderness ranger, thinning crew foreman, wildlife technician, and wildlife biologist. I'd worked in eight states and had developed the wildlife management program on the fourth largest Indian reservation in the country, the San Carlos Apache Reservation in Arizona.

About the only time I wasn't working or studying was the three months I spent horseback, drifting along with the tumbling tumbleweed. Restless at 24, I bought two horses in Benson, Arizona, learned how to tie a diamond hitch, and rode north. Given the rapid economic development of the American west, I was probably one of the last to make a solo pack trip from Arizona to Idaho.

So I could never have imagined that one day a keyboard plunker in the Washington, DC beltway would accuse me of lacking horse sense! Yet that's what happened at FWS headquarters. This fellow—let's call him Dick Schultz[5]—had spent some time in the field and thought he had a monopoly

---

[5] Fictitious names of FWS employees are used herein, except in a few, complimentary cases.

on the word "practical." He liked to denigrate scholars as ivory tower eggheads, no matter what they'd done outside academia.

Typical of FWS "leaders" at the beginning of the 21st century, Schultz was embarrassingly ignorant about the biggest challenges facing the Service, including economic growth, climate change, and genetically modified organisms. Once, in a meeting on the issue of sea-level rise—easily the greatest threat to coastal wetlands by then—Schultz conflated centimeters with millimeters while dismissing the threat. We'd been discussing the prospect of nine centimeters (3 ½ inches) of sea-level rise, and Schultz gaffed, "What's nine centimeters? Like this?" projecting his thumb and index finger a few millimeters apart. Bill Wilen, chief of the National Wetlands Inventory and a Ph.D. ecologist, was present as well, and was flabbergasted by the error and dismissiveness of Schultz.

In another meeting, Schultz insisted that glyphosate—the active and controversial ingredient in the herbicide Roundup—was "glyphosphate," even though he'd probably overseen the application of Roundup many times, over tens of thousands of acres. Presumably he'd read a warning label or two, as required of pesticide applicators, but Schultz was such a fan of Big Ag, he might as well have been reading the old propaganda poster, "DDT is Good for Me."

Schultz's idea of "practical" was hook-and-bullet wildlife management, especially growing corn and soybeans (with the help of "glyphosphate") for ducks and geese. He was "practical" as a bureaucrat too, saying "yes" to anything from above, and "no" to anything from below that would threaten to make waves. Naturally enough he ended up at headquarters, where he became one of my first gag-orderers. Taxpayers supported his fat salary for decades until he finally retired to a life of hunting and fishing in Minnesota.

Those inclined to defend Schultz would note that he was regularly exposed to the influence of the "Bible Club," the 4 o'clock beer drinkers from Fish and Wildlife headquarters. The Bible Club was central to gag-order sociology, to be explored in Chapter 6. First, though, a little more background…

I'd seen a lot of wild country before I signed on with FWS, but I'd also seen massive clearcuts in the Pacific Northwest, pivot agriculture in the Great Plains, overgrazing in the Great Basin, open-pit mining in the Southwest, commercial fishing on the Bering Sea, and the rampant regional development around Seattle, Dallas, and Phoenix. I'd seen it all firsthand and close up. Even the place I grew up—once a haven for deer and pheasants—had become an unrecognizable neighborhood of Green Bay, Wisconsin. I hadn't yet thought in terms of "economic growth," but to me it was clear that way too much wildlife habitat was being lost, and way too fast.

One place that still had a lot of wildlife habitat was the San Carlos Apache Reservation in Arizona, where I was hired to develop the wildlife management program.[6] For a wildlife biologist like me, there was no comparison with "the Rez." At the time, my specialty (from my master's research) was elk, and the San Carlos elk had the biggest antlers and the wildest elk rut in the world, all amid a spectacular diversity of "charismatic megafauna." In addition to elk were mule deer, Coues whitetail, Rocky Mountain bighorn sheep, desert bighorn, pronghorn antelope, javelina, black bears, mountain lions, and huge flocks of wild turkeys roaming the plains, mountains, and canyons. And that was only the megafauna. Surrounded by ecological diversity from lower Sonoran Desert all the way up to the mixed conifer forests above the ponderosa zone, I felt like a modern-day John Muir as I explored every mountain and valley, every habitat and niche.

I was extremely grateful to the San Carlos Apache Tribe for the chance to serve on their spectacular reservation. I was in wildlife biology heaven, and for years I regretted ever leaving it. But something had been bothering me, making me restless again. In addition to the tribal government, which I worked for, the *federal* government had a heavy presence. Much of the reservation was a de facto wilderness area because almost all the Apaches lived in the tiny towns of San Carlos, Peridot, and Bylas. The remaining Apaches were cowboys and ranchers, loggers and miners, sparsely populating the deserts, woodlands, and forests. You could easily spend days or even weeks without encountering another soul.

I always had the impression that the Apaches, certainly the ones I met, liked their reservation big and wild. The main reasons were practical: the unfettered hunting opportunities that were integral to Apache culture, the tribal economy, and, simply put, food on the table. Too, there was a palpable tribal pride in recalling the days of Geronimo, leading his would-be captors up the dramatic topography of the Nantac Rim, a place that seemed lost in time. There along the rim, in places like Soldier's Hole and up on the broad Natanes Plateau, the great-great grandkids of Geronimo hunted for the deer and elk descended from those that sustained Geronimo himself. Not being a tribal member, I can't say for sure, but Soldier's Hole seemed sacred for a

---

[6] I was hired in 1988 to develop the wildlife management program for the San Carlos Apache Tribe and its 1.8 million-acre reservation. I spent three years at this task and then took over as the director of the San Carlos Recreation and Wildlife Department until 1993.

tribe that was the last to surrender to an upstart United States and its vision of manifest destiny.

Yet the Bureau of Indian Affairs—an agency in the Department of the Interior—was busy as a bee, developing roads and timber sales throughout the reservation. The timber sales, especially, were often destructive of wildlife habitats, including elk, turkey, and Mexican spotted owl habitats. It was ironic because the wildlife was extremely valuable to the tribe—economically as well as culturally—while the timber sales were barely economical. The BIA had to subsidize many of the forestry activities on the reservation as well as the tribal sawmill.

We all wanted to help the tribal economy, but developing roads and timber sales at the expense of wildlife was the wrong way to go about it. I knew that if I were in the BIA, I'd be making different decisions about allocating resources among forestry, range, and wildlife programs. I'd be allocating far more funding to wildlife conservation, with the result being fewer timber sales, less road development, lighter cattle grazing, and more sustainable wildlife populations.

It turns out there were sympathetic minds in the BIA, too, especially at the San Carlos Agency. The problem was, they were constrained by political and bureaucratic decisions handed down from BIA headquarters in Washington, DC. Little by little, I started thinking about taking more responsibility for wildlife conservation at the national level, or at least trying to.

I also started thinking about the problems caused by misguided efforts to stimulate the economy. "Why stimulate the economy if you're messing up what you love the most?" I wondered. "Doesn't it defeat the purpose?" I often discussed these questions with one of the tribal wildlife commissioners, John Stevens, who wholeheartedly agreed and elaborated profusely.

Unlike the political appointees, though, I had no connections whatsoever in the Washington, DC offices of anything (other than the thinnest of files at the Internal Revenue Service). My only hope for a job in DC was yet another stint in school. I had to broaden my horizons beyond wildlife management and learn more about conservation biology, landscape ecology, and climate change. Plus, I had to supplement these natural sciences with courses in American government, Congress, the bureaucracy, the Supreme Court, policy analysis—anything that would give me a leg up on conservation affairs at the national level. I wanted to go to DC with a toolbox full of concepts I could put to use in conservation policy development, and with a license to do so in the form of a doctorate.

I enrolled at the University of Arizona and pursued a broad major in "renewable natural resources studies," which allowed for a rich mixture of courses, accompanied by a minor in political science. I sought to develop a graduate committee with academic firepower. With Paul Krausman (my major professor) and Helen Ingram, I had the guidance of prominent scholars in the worlds of wildlife conservation and political science, respectively, plus three other accomplished faculty. I specialized in natural resources policy analysis from a technical and political perspective. I put it all together with the aforementioned analysis of the Endangered Species Act. The whole program entailed 81 credits, which I took seriously enough for a 4.0 grade-point average.

Noting a 4.0 GPA might seem boastful (and embarrassing, if you prefer modesty), but I think the information is entirely useful in the present context. It's an indication of due diligence and intensive exploration of a curriculum. Discerning readers are entitled to know that I'd done my homework, literally. They'll be left to wonder if the same can be said about some of the other characters appearing herein.

In any event, a Ph.D. is no guarantee of a job in natural resources, much less a high-paying one. In some ways the Ph.D. can be a curse. You're "overqualified" for 95 percent of American jobs, even if you'd gladly take 75 percent of them (and seemingly already did the other 25 percent of jobs to finance your way into graduate school). The jobs you're not overqualified for are highly competitive.

Furthermore, the supply of wildlife-related jobs is especially limited because most of these jobs are found in an eroding public sector, not an expanding private sector. Yet the demand for such jobs is intense because many people—especially vigorous young graduates entering the workforce—love the outdoors and the drama of spectacular wildlife. Can you imagine, for example, trying to get a decent-paying job (as opposed to a volunteer position) working in the Northern Rockies with grizzly bears? Better get to work on your Ph.D., and be prepared to spend a considerable chunk of your life jockeying for the position!

In my case, after wrapping up my dissertation, I spent approximately a third of my time at a low-paying, nasty job with a consulting firm. I was sent out on foot in front of a bulldozer—a D9 Caterpillar—picking up rattlesnakes and horned toads and moving them out of harm's way to "mitigate" for the excavating of an 18-hole golf course. It's hard to imagine a job—D9 on your tail in the sweltering Arizona sun—more replete with dust, sweat, and the

800-Pound Gorilla. And just down the road from the Amphitheater School District, no less, with its cactus ferruginous pygmy owls.

I spent another third of my time on two books. One of them didn't take much original writing, because it was a conversion of my dissertation into a book on the Endangered Species Act (published by Johns Hopkins University Press in 2001). The other one, however, started out where the dissertation left off, focusing on the steady state economy as the sustainable alternative to economic growth. This book entailed postdoctoral studies in economics, history, and psychology (for insights into consumer behavior). I was also determined to put it all into plain language for the masses, so it took a lot of linguistic massaging. The title was *Shoveling Fuel for a Runaway Train*, the runaway train being the growing economy. Those doing the shoveling included economists, conspicuous consumers, and policymakers hell-bent on economic growth.

I spent the final third of my time applying for permanent, full-time jobs. I was determined to make a difference for conservation at the national level by *applying* the education and experience I'd invested so much in, not simply building upon it in academia.

To put it another way, I'd made a decision to spend the academic capital I'd accumulated rather than accumulate ever more of it. Frankly, it was a difficult, conscientious decision, and my political science advisor, Helen Ingram, advised me not to do it. I would be sacrificing intellectual development and academic reputation for the mere prospect—no guarantees—of influencing conservation policy. It was a gamble and a tough decision, but I went for it.

More than anything, the decision was a *practical* one. I was used to getting things done after assessing the obstacles. Now, I felt there was a tiny bottleneck obstructing the vast store of scientific knowledge from reaching the natural resource managers of our federal agencies. I wasn't sure why, but I wanted to "get in there" and open up that bottleneck. Therefore the focus of my job search was the federal government in Washington, DC; in particular a job in policy analysis or policy development for one of the natural resource agencies such as the U.S. Forest Service, U.S. Park Service, or Bureau of Land Management. However, since I was a certified wildlife biologist concerned especially with wildlife conservation, the agency at the top of my list was the U.S. Fish and Wildlife Service.

In late 1998, a job announcement appeared for a "Conservation Biologist," with a starting date of January, 1999, and duty station of Arlington, Virginia. The position was in the headquarters of the National Wildlife

Refuge System, the land management arm of the FWS. The Refuge System was all the rage in the Department of the Interior, due to the passage of the National Wildlife Refuge System Improvement Act of 1997, the belated but strong organic act of the Refuge System.[7] The Refuge Improvement Act was clear, comprehensive legislation providing a unifying mission for refuges, core management principles, and key administrative adjustments.

But what really caught my attention in the position description was the duties, which were broad, big-picture, and exciting. They seemed made-to-order for my freshly minted diploma, broad major, emphasis on conservation biology, and policy analysis background. The whole purpose of the position was "to serve as the focal point for major management, legislative, and regulatory activities related to the Refuge System."

Ponder that for a moment, please: "to serve as the focal point for major management, legislative, and regulatory activities related to the Refuge System." I couldn't have written a better position description for the job I wanted.

Next, the position required "an integrated knowledge of concepts and techniques of community ecology, biogeography, zoology, and sustainable development." It also called for "comprehensive professional knowledge of the principles, theories, concepts, and practical realities of conservation biology and landscape ecology," to "serve as the technical authority to address complex environmental problems and issues affecting the [Refuge System] and the nation's ecosystems in innovative and imaginative ways," and to "project trends and future needs related to biological diversity." I checked off the phrases one by one, enthusiastically matching them with courses from my curriculum, jobs from my past, and in some cases both.

As if that weren't enough, the conservation biologist was to serve as the "lead in developing national goals and evaluating key refuge programs" while maintaining a "current knowledge of conservation biology system principles and how they relate to the [Refuge System], emerging national priorities and developing critical issues."

The announcement acknowledged, "Many issues encountered are very sensitive politically with diverse interest groups representing varied opinions, such as subsistence, access, fishing, hunting, economic use, and other land management issues." To prevent undue political tampering or micromanagement, supervision was to be "broad and limited to matters of policy, budget, and highly controversial matters." Similarly, guidelines were to be "broad

---

[7] R.L. Fischman, 2003. *The National Wildlife Refuges.*

in nature" and the conservation biologist would "exercise a high degree of judgement and initiative."

It was a match made in heaven—*the perfect job*—and it started out precisely as portrayed. That lasted for one year and part of the second, and it was downhill from there. Slowly downhill at first, and then (to borrow a line from C.W. McCall) like a rocket sled on rails. Eventually, the only aspect of the job that still fit the position description was: "must be able to work under conditions of mental and some physical stress." My carpal tunnels can attest to the latter; my loss of smile to the former.

But back in the late 1990s, just as the Refuge System was all the rage in the Department of the Interior, conservation biology was the rage in the biological sciences. Conservation biology had arisen as an antidote to the narrow thinking that permeated wildlife science in academia and wildlife management in government agencies. It was designed to expand the horizons of scientists and managers beyond hook-and-bullet species to the conservation of biological diversity at large, most notably the complete collection of native species. In a sense, conservation biology was the civil rights movement of natural resource management.

The analogy with the civil rights movement is a bit more nuanced than it may first seem. Not only did conservation biology emphasize the protection of all species; it also brought in students and scholars who had otherwise struggled to find a niche in the wildlife profession. For example, in the 1970s and 1980s inner-city girls who had never toted a shotgun had to endure culture shock in a typical wildlife management program. Even if they made it through the curriculum, they were highly unlikely to land a position in hook-and-bullet wildlife management.

Similarly, boys like E.O. Wilson, growing up fascinated by insects, wound up in university zoology departments far removed from the agencies that managed millions of acres that would have benefited from their brilliance. Meanwhile, minority students from tropical countries oblivious to North American hunting and fishing society were also at a major disadvantage in the wildlife curriculum of American colleges and universities. In academia, wildlife management was a "good ol' boys club" if ever there was one. This problem of exclusivity was greatly alleviated by the rise of conservation biology.

By pure happenstance, my education and career grew in tandem with conservation biology. At the University of Wisconsin in the 1980s, my undergraduate advisor was Stanley Temple, one of the founders of the movement. Growing up hunting and fishing, I was actually attracted to the hook-and-bullet occupations myself, but I also "got it" when it came to the broader goals of conservation biology. In fact, it seemed to me the wildlife management profession had gotten away from *its own* roots, because in the 1930s Aldo Leopold, the father of wildlife management, had called for a "land ethic" designed to protect the balance of nature, including all its denizens. One need only read *A Sand County Almanac* to be reminded of the "conservation biology" at the core of Leopold's philosophy.

But by the 1990s a new movement with its own professional society, journal, textbooks, and jobs was needed to counteract the hook-and-bullet approach and get us back to the Leopoldian vision. Therefore, the Society for Conservation Biology, the journal *Conservation Biology*, and jobs such as "conservation biologist" came into being.

The easiest way to distinguish conservation biology from traditional wildlife ecology and management is the emphasis on conserving biological diversity, or "biodiversity." Biodiversity is typically thought of in terms of numbers of species ("species richness") but can also be thought of in terms of diversity within species, such as genetic diversity, and diversity beyond species, such as the variety of ecosystems found across the landscape.

While these various topics and emphases have helped to distinguish conservation biology from hook-and-bullet wildlife management, they're not the truly decisive difference. The *big* difference is that conservation biology, as originally conceived and at its purest, is truly an interdisciplinary and even a transdisciplinary pursuit, transcending the boundaries of traditional disciplines such as biology, zoology, and ecology.

In other words, conservation biology requires *whatever knowledge it takes* to conserve biodiversity. This is the art in the science of conservation biology: identifying what it takes. For some species, it might be a knowledge of chemistry. For others, it could be a knowledge of hydrology. For others still, it's a knowledge of genetics, pollutants, competition from invasive species, etc.

For many species, it's a knowledge of microeconomics, especially in capitalist economies where market forces compete with public policies. How do we ascertain the value of a pollinator or a pest-controlling predator to the human economy, such that the public and policymakers develop more appreciation for these species? Which markets are relevant to the species? What financial incentives would help landowners to maintain these species' habitats?

And guess what knowledge is required for conserving biodiversity at large, all species together, the whole "economy of nature?" If you guessed that it's all about the 800-Pound Gorilla, I urge you to teach school, write books, or run for office! I'd especially urge you to sign on with FWS. (Unfortunately, they're not yet hiring on the basis of grasping the big picture, so be prepared for a frustrating ride.)

If you're a student, use your highlighter and mark this well: *Biodiversity conservation is all about conquering our addiction to economic growth.* As we move from the conservation of individual species to the entire collection of species, we're moving from microeconomic issues to macroeconomic. To put it in terms of conservation biology: "Due to the tremendous breadth of the human niche, the human economy grows at the competitive exclusion of nonhuman species in the aggregate."[8] To put it in terms of economic policy, biodiversity conservation requires the establishment of a steady state economy. And to put it in lay terms, you can't have your cake and eat it too.

Some of the leaders in conservation biology sensed this from the start, although very few of them developed the expertise to describe it in policy-relevant terms. So that's where I finally found my niche, a niche I called "ecological macroeconomics" (a phrase that spread, although not in FWS). Conservation biology requires a heavy dose of ecological macroeconomics, because otherwise it will amount to an exercise in futility. As long as the overriding policy goal is economic growth, biodiversity will continue to decline.

And this, taxpayers and politicians, is the dirty little secret among the "leadership" at U.S. Fish and Wildlife Service headquarters. They're having a ball—visiting refuges, throwing parties at the National Conservation Training Center,[9] and even travelling the world—all while claiming credit for a species here and a project there. Meanwhile Rome is burning.

And they know it.

---

[8] Czech, B., P.R. Krausman, and P.K. Devers. 2000. Economic associations among causes of species endangerment in the United States. *BioScience* 50(7):593.

[9] The National Conservation Training Center, or NCTC, was a pork-barrel project of Robert C. Byrd, the long-time Republican senator from West Virginia. A gem among Fish and Wildlife Service properties, NCTC is a learning campus with park-like surroundings near Shepherdstown, West Virginia. It includes a buffet-style café run by gourmet chefs, a bar serving beer and free popcorn, and a top-notch fitness center among the laboratories, auditoriums, trails, and lodges. It has been used for high-level government meetings, such as when President Clinton made it the "temporary White House" during a Middle East peace summit in 2000. Fish and Wildlife Service leadership, especially in the National Wildlife Refuge System, use NCTC as a home away from home, continually shuttling from the Washington, DC beltway to their favorite lodges on the NCTC campus..

3

A TALE OF TWO BRIEFINGS

There were at least 267 reasons I landed the conservation biologist job; one for each expensive credit of university education. The 81 credits from the University of Arizona alone included topics from molecular evolution to global change, plus the public policy curriculum from the political science minor. There's no arrogance about this, just the academic facts, which become more relevant as the story progresses.

What should really have distinguished my resume, though, was the niche I'd developed in ecological macroeconomics. *Shoveling Fuel for a Runaway Train* hadn't come out yet, but I had already been advancing the topic within the wildlife profession.

Those were the days—prior to Facebook, Twitter, and Google Groups—of the email "listserv." The Wildlife Society (TWS) had an active listserv, and I was an active participant. So when I organized a symposium for the 1997 TWS conference in Buffalo, New York, it was a crowded affair that instantly and substantially expanded my network. Pursuant to the symposium, I published a paper in the *Wildlife Society Bulletin*—the trade journal for wildlife professionals—establishing the theoretical basis for the conflict between economic growth and wildlife conservation.[10]

In the journal, on the listserv, and at the annual conferences for several years, I pushed a policy statement on economic growth for consideration by TWS membership and its governing Council. The 800-Pound Gorilla rapidly became one of the hottest topics in The Wildlife Society. The policy statement described the "fundamental conflict between economic growth and wildlife conservation" and was eventually passed, despite the determined efforts of timber industry employees to derail it.[11]

---

[10] Czech, B. 2000. Economic growth as the limiting factor for wildlife conservation. *Wildlife Society Bulletin* 28(1):4-14.

[11] To get the position adopted I literally had to debate—formally—one of the more

In other words, the U.S. Fish and Wildlife Service, *especially* its leadership in headquarters, should have been well aware of my background in ecological macroeconomics and how it tied in to the duties of the conservation biologist position. More importantly than my expertise, they should have been well aware of the topics. As I soon discovered, however, such was not the case. The leadership of the National Wildlife Refuge System, in particular, was too busy touring the refuges and calculating their per-diem payments (see Chapter 11).

What went on in The Wildlife Society was of little concern to Refuge System chiefs, who cared even less about the Society for Conservation Biology, Ecological Society of America, and American Fisheries Society. The International Society for Ecological Economics and the U.S. Society for Ecological Economics were unheard of by them. What got published in journals such as *Conservation Biology* was Greek to Refuge System leadership; *Ecological Economics* may as well have been published in Martian.

This was disconcerting but not entirely surprising. The exigencies of wildlife management kept the field biologists, at least, out of the libraries and conference halls. Also, the Fish and Wildlife Service was one of the more underfunded agencies, due largely to Congress's reluctance to unleash the full regulatory power of the Endangered Species Act. That said, it was surprising that, with all the bright, motivated, hard-working, high-level graduates, many of them trudging in front of the proverbial D9 Caterpillar, Refuge System headquarters was populated by SUV-driving bureaucrats who had never done much other than work on a refuge or two. In fact, a lot of the staff hadn't spent any time in the field *or* achieved anything of note in academia.

The Realty Division was illustrative. This division had a tradition of "conservative" activism, where "conserve" was lost in the activism. A realty chief by the name of Alberres obstinately opposed a Department of the Interior policy on energy conservation, which called for turning off the lights when leaving the office. Alberres stunned the biologists by arguing in a staff meeting, "We have the right to leave the lights on." I often wondered what the hell that meant—the "right" to leave the lights on—but he left them on for sure, rightly or wrongly.

---

prominent timber industry biologists, Jonathan Haufler, at one of The Wildlife Society's annual conferences. Haufler took the stance that "there is no conflict between economic growth and wildlife conservation." All the feedback I got indicated that he was roundly defeated. To Haufler's credit, he abandoned the win-win metaphysics and was eventually elected president of The Wildlife Society.

Alberres also favored paying half a million dollars per acre for Florida beach property, which was imminently threatened by sea-level rise. For the same money, we could have acquired stable, secure refuge lands, upland and inland, *and* protected the beaches (from basic, direct threats at least) via the Endangered Species Act.

Alberres actually liked to boast about advancing to his chief position without the need for a graduate degree. But taxpayers were cheated with Alberres, because FWS could easily have found a savvy scholar with graduate degrees in economics *and* ecology, *and* with a background in realty; that is, someone perfect for the job of realty chief. In fact, a short two blocks from headquarters, The Nature Conservancy employed these types of experts by the busload. Instead, Alberres was hand-picked and groomed by a politically aligned predecessor. His tenure with the FWS bordered on "waste, fraud, and abuse," as he fought tooth and nail to preclude cost considerations from land acquisition.

When I introduced the concept of "conservation return on investment," Alberres fought against it. Numerous other FWS chiefs agreed with me but did nothing about it. Conservation return on investment was never adopted as a land acquisition criterion, despite a request by Public Employees for Environmental Responsibility to explain why not.[12]

But that's how it worked in the FWS; many divisions and programs didn't require a rigorous academic background, a conservation ethic, or even a basic sense of responsibility.

For some agency jobs—facilities management, financial operations, and records management come to mind—it's true that academic achievement is outweighed by experience and demonstrated proficiency. Taken together, these jobs comprise the general matrix of government operations, as opposed to mission-specific programs such as migratory bird management,

---

[12] In 2011, Public Employees for Environmental Responsibility (PEER) issued a request for information, pursuant to the Freedom of Information Act (FOIA), pertaining to the Land Acquisition Priority System, which was used at the time to target lands for acquisition using the Land and Water Conservation Fund. PEER asked if the Refuge System used cost considerations (as well as benefits) in prioritizing lands for acquisition, in accordance with several policies. PEER also asked if climate change was being considered. In both cases, the Refuge System was remiss, but bought time by suggesting the issues were still being analyzed, and that LAPS would be modified to accommodate concerns about costs and climate change. By 2017, LAPS was defunct—replaced by another pure-benefits system called TRACT—and had never evolved to account for costs or climate change.

conservation biology, and fisheries conservation. Academic titles are and should be optional in the "matrix."

For most of the matrix workers, the conservation ethic is optional, too. It's definitely a bonus when FWS co-workers share a concern for wildlife conservation, because it's conducive to camaraderie. That said, when it comes to, say, information technology, we want geeks managing our computer systems and fending off the hackers.

What frustrated many of the biologists, though, was that Refuge System programs in realty, public relations, and even planning and policy were populated by specialists with no graduate credentials, much less in wildlife science or management. These are programs where a conservation ethic is of the essence, and a nuanced one at that. (Far beyond, for example, the common sense of turning the lights off.)

The Refuge System would have done far better hiring Ph.D. biologists and training them in the straightforward occupations of realty transaction, public relations, planning, and policy development. Instead, you might say we had "realtors," "marketers," and aspiring "developers" and "politicians"—and not even renowned ones—handling key conservation programs. We had realty specialists who didn't understand ecosystem classification, public affairs specialists who didn't know the difference between extinct and extirpated, and planners better suited to county commissions than the National Wildlife Refuge System. The pool of bright, talented, impassioned Ph.D. biologists is an expansive one, and many would jump at the chance to handle realty, public relations, and planning and policy affairs for the leading federal wildlife agency.

Professional leadership for a mission-specific agency should overlap substantially with academic achievement, including a leading presence in scholarly journals. Therefore I was shocked at the paucity of publications that could be attributed to Refuge System headquarters. There was a bit of gray literature here and there, but peer-reviewed publications by Refuge System chiefs could be counted on the toes of a sloth; a two-toed sloth at that. Yet Refuge System leadership was fond of touting its "scientifically sound" management.

Luckily for me—at least in terms of getting the job—there did happen to be (in 1999) a small cohort of smart, progressive, open-minded professionals at Refuge System headquarters, and they happened to be right above and around the new conservation biologist position. Most notably, the chief was Rick Coleman, who had developed a strong interest in the steady state economy while serving as a refuge manager at San Francisco Bay National Wildlife Refuge. He was exceedingly rare in that respect; no one else in headquarters had even a passing knowledge of the topic, although a few would develop some knowledge in subsequent years.

Rick Coleman was a pleasure to work for. He was bright and articulate, with bachelor's and master's degrees from Michigan State and a Ph.D. from Penn State. He was fully conversant with a broad range of wildlife management issues. He was an outstanding networker, fabulous public speaker, and inspiring leader. Perhaps most importantly, he was encouraging to everyone he met. Coleman deserves a lot of credit for the outstanding morale that permeated Refuge System headquarters at the time.

Meanwhile, not long after I arrived at headquarters, I attended a social function of FWS leaders. Who did I encounter but the fellow I'd met at the public hearing in Tucson. I probed my memory, "What was the name again?" Ah yes, Dan Crasche. His eyes opened just a trace wider as I walked up to shake his hand. And why not? I had challenged his win-win rhetoric before the masses in Tucson, and suddenly there I was in DC, shaking his hand, reintroducing myself as the newest addition to headquarters staff.

It quickly became apparent that Crasche's thoughts revolved around "trust species," which was semi-legal jargon for the species managed "in trust" for the American people. Trust species included migratory birds, certain types of wide-ranging fishes,[13] federally listed threatened and endangered species, and a few marine mammals. The concept of "trust species" was a halfway house between hook-and-bullet wildlife management and conservation biology.

The word "biodiversity" was also in Crasche's vocabulary, but only as a collection of pieces, not in the sense of an assembled puzzle. As for ecological economics? That was still foreign territory to Crasche. He was a trust-species man infused with the Clintonian win-win rhetoric that "there is no conflict between growing the economy and protecting the environment."[14]

---

[13] FWS has jurisdiction over certain anadromous fishes—species that split their life cycles between saltwater and freshwater—and wide-ranging interior (freshwater) species.

[14] Early in my FWS career, a mid-level manager took me aside to inform me that, several years prior (during the mid 1990's), a small team of Clintonian appointees had been making the rounds among natural resource agency headquarters. These high-level appointees instructed lesser appointees and managers on how to talk about the relationship between economic growth and environmental protection. The bottom line was to persuade the public that "there is no conflict between growing the economy and protecting the environment." This propaganda campaign would help explain the behavior of Dan Crasche and other FWS appointees at the time. However, the campaign is relegated to a footnote because I did not

Nevertheless, it felt good to be among these higher-level conservation professionals, even including Crasche. This was a group in a solid position—with the benefit of taxpayer resources—to help raise public awareness of the trade-off between economic growth and wildlife conservation. The fact that they themselves might first have to learn about the trade-off was a challenge I was prepared to face.

Rick Coleman helped by arranging for me to speak at one of the weekly directorate briefings. The directorate included the Director, eight regional directors, and various assistant directors in charge of national programs such as fisheries, migratory birds, and the Refuge System. There were 15-20 people at the briefing, all of them in relatively high-level leadership positions. My goal was to introduce them to the ecological economics of wildlife conservation. The focus would be the conflict between economic growth and wildlife conservation.

The Director was Jamie Clark, and she had instituted Tuesday-morning briefings that were focused on technical issues with crucial implications for the FWS. I sincerely thanked her and the rest of the directorate for the opportunity to address them. I said that, in my opinion, the U.S. Fish and Wildlife Service was the most important conservation organization in the world. I told them that if we were to lead the way in raising awareness of the trade-off between economic growth and wildlife conservation, it would catalyze a tremendous amount of latent energy toward the same end. It made a good first impression, stirred people a bit, and was a sincere observation on my part.

But first, the agency had to develop some expertise in the matter, starting at the top. Otherwise, it would continue to send political appointees to public hearings to regurgitate the win-win rhetoric that "there is no conflict…" Therefore, the focus of my presentation was the theoretical and empirical evidence for the conflict between economic growth and wildlife conservation. I also gave a thumbnail sketch of why so many people had been led to think there was no such conflict, and I concluded with an overview of the steady state economy as the sustainable alternative to growth.

Jamie Clark was the first person to comment following the presentation, and announced in an animated voice, "This has been the most intellectually stimulating briefing we've had!" She elaborated a bit about how challenging it also was. She invited me to come back with a follow-up about what

---

personally witness it, nor did I hear about it from any other source. I have no reason to doubt the source, however, and every reason to believe his account.

we—FWS—might be able to do about the conflict between economic growth and wildlife conservation.

Everything was going according to plan! The prospects for difference-making were palpable. My faith in American democracy—in particular the civil service aspect—was lifted. The tens of thousands of dollars I'd spent on graduate-level education seemed to be paying off quickly; the Ph.D. was looking like a worthwhile license indeed. More importantly, I felt we could make a huge and long-lasting difference in the way the United States—the most powerful nation on Earth—perceived and approached the topic of economic growth.

I immediately set to work on the return engagement, which was to occur about five months later. My goal for the next briefing was to compel the directorate to *do something* about the conflict between economic growth and wildlife conservation, not just ponder it.

Of course "*doing* something" can be a loaded term. By "doing something," I didn't mean the directorate would go out and start monkey-wrenching powerlines or picketing the Federal Reserve. What I meant was the FWS had a leading role to play—quite possibly *the* leading role—in raising public awareness of the conflict between economic growth and environmental protection. The reason I felt the Service was so important was because the conflict between economic growth and environmental protection is most evident with the issue of wildlife conservation. GDP goes up and species become imperiled in the process. And species are like the canaries in the environmental coalmine. When you see them becoming imperiled one after another, you know you have a serious environmental problem.

What hope was there unless the American public and polity had a thorough grasp of the conflict? And this was no tree-hugger issue. The most immediate and evident conflict was between economic growth and environmental protection, yes, but furthermore the environment is the foundation of the economy. The economy, meanwhile, is central to a civilized society. Therefore in the bigger picture, the conflict was between economic growth and economic sustainability, national security, and international stability.

When I returned in 2000 for my follow-up presentation to the directorate, I told them there were four intensity levels to consider: passive, implicit, defensive, and aggressive. The passive approach entailed something quite simple and easy, namely, abandoning the old "win-win" rhetoric. In other words, we wouldn't necessarily tell the public about the conflict between economic growth and wildlife conservation, but we would stop opiating the masses with claims of "no conflict."

The implicit approach was designed to lay the groundwork for defensive and aggressive approaches, but subtly and gradually. The method was simple: training FWS employees in the basic principles of ecological economics and especially the conflict between growth and conservation. We would also systematically employ the jargon of ecological economics, such as "natural capital" and "ecosystem services," in our public communications, getting these phrases and their implications into the public lexicon. We would show our support for steady-state organizations and events, such as the U.S. Society for Ecological Economics and its annual conference. And, though we would not publish any literature criticizing the national goal of economic growth, we would allow the display of such literature in our public buildings (including, for example, the visitor centers that occupy most of our 568 national wildlife refuges).

The defensive approach entailed explicit economic language. For example, when we drafted documents describing the threats to endangered species, we would use phrases such as "economic growth" or at least "economic activities" instead of the patently obvious and politically impotent "human activities" to summarize industrial development, logging, mining, ranching, commercial fishing, etc. At public hearings on endangered species, we would hearken back to the opening sentence of the Endangered Species Act, in which Congress "finds and declares" that "various species of fish, wildlife, and plants in the United States have been rendered extinct as a consequence of economic growth."

With the aggressive approach, we would take frequent opportunities to proclaim the impossibility of long-term wildlife conservation in a growing economy, challenge the assumptions and conclusions of perpetual growth theory, and deny the continued appropriateness of economic growth. We would endeavor to get the phrase "steady state economy" into the American vocabulary, so the majority could rally around the concept as the sustainable alternative to growth. We would exhort citizens to lower consumption in the private sector—as Aldo Leopold had—while in the public sector we would encourage policy reform toward a steady state. We would, essentially, champion the steady state economy as a macroeconomic policy goal.

I recommended to the directorate that fine day in 2000 that we start with the implicit approach. But then I took a calculated risk that turned out to backfire. I handed out some mock FWS "fact sheets" as an example of an outreach tool that could be used, for example in the visitor centers of our national wildlife refuges. Following a few basics on the process of economic growth on one hand and the habitat needs of wildlife on the other, the fact sheet concluded with the following:

> The earth has a limited capacity for ourselves and our goods and services. A huge economy and little wildlife, or a moderate economy and much wildlife: the choice is ours.

I emphasized that the mock-up was simply an example, and not even an example I'd approve of. Rather, it was an example of the "aggressive" approach I recommended *against* at that early stage.

Why hand out an example that even I didn't condone? The strategy had three components. One was to illustrate that even the "aggressive" approach wouldn't have to seem obnoxious or crazy. The words of the fact sheet were based on a sober assessment of the relationship between economic growth and wildlife conservation. The words were just the facts, with no "fake news."

The second component of the strategy was to demonstrate that I was, in fact, being ultra-reasonable in recommending an implicit approach. It was like having the directorate ponder the challenge of a 16-foot pole vault, then setting the bar at 4 feet.

The third component was to give folks a vision of the types of outreach we might be headed for at some future time. And frankly I was hedging my bets because, for all I knew, it was possible the Director herself was ready and waiting to "go there" already.

After a quick discussion of the mock fact sheet, I went on to address the "avenues of delivery" we might use: academic articles, public literature (including fact sheets), speeches, press releases, meetings, and eventually congressional testimony. I concluded with the topic of in-house training and proposed the assignment of a few positions to the program.

As with the first seminar, the Director was interested and enthused about the prospects for such a program. As for what I might do to follow up, she directed me for the time being to coordinate with her speech writer. Meanwhile, she and her staff would be discussing the potential for a steady-state program. She concluded, "I encourage you to keep bugging us about this."

Somebody beat me to the bugging, however, and put a bigger bug than mine squarely in the ear of Jamie Clark. I always suspected a squinting woman from the Office of Legislative Affairs, the only person who never smiled during the entire presentation. Instead, for the duration of my talk she looked riled, roiled, and raring to debate, as if she'd recently been indoctrinated in perpetual growth theory at the Mercatus Center. Maybe she had been![15] She wasn't a member of the directorate, per se, but evidently a trusted advisor to the Director.

Within 24 hours I had a scolding and scathing email from this antagonistic advisor, who unscrupulously copied everyone at the briefing, plus various supervisory personnel in my chain of command! To her, at least, the content of the mock fact sheet was explosive enough to be avoided like a stick of dynamite, and more importantly, I'd failed to include the word "DRAFT" in big bold letters. Now she was warning me—and an absurdly large population of chiefs—what political death we'd suffer if one of these fact sheets made it out to the wrong party.

I'm probably not the only public servant to find out the hard way that overlooking the word "DRAFT" can come back to haunt you. I had gotten in a rush, printing the fact sheet literally minutes before I left for the briefing. I remember thinking, "I forgot the word 'DRAFT,' but they'll obviously know it's a draft and I'll tell them to be safe." To be extra safe indeed, I assured the attendees that the mock-up wasn't going anywhere outside the briefing. There was no way it could have, without being signed off by the Director.

But that wasn't good enough for the advisor, who was instantly out for blood. Her email was the most reactionary I have ever seen (directed to me at least). It cost me a fistful of political capital, too early in my headquarters career, and undoubtedly caused the directorate undue angst.

I'll never know exactly what possessed the advisor to craft such a harmful email and copy it to so many. She never discussed it with me. Her email seemed designed to discredit me and to impress upon the recipients her ability to "protect" the Service from political harm. It was a Machiavellian move, and it must have scared the enthusiasm out of Jamie Clark. Her once-positive attitude toward the steady-state program was transformed overnight. The steady-state program was down for the count, and I was left staggering out of the loop.

For that matter, so was Jamie Clark, after the hanging chads were counted and George W. Bush claimed the White House.

---

[15] See *Dark Money* (Mayer 2016). Pro-growth, anti-government disciples of the Koch-funded Mercatus Center (of George Mason University) are shockingly well-distributed around the U.S. I met one while working for the Fish and Wildlife Service; he was employed (ironically enough) as a civil servant in the U.S. Geological Survey.

In my opinion, Clark missed her chance to go out in a blaze of glory, or at least a blaze of relevance, by issuing a press release about the fundamental conflict between economic growth and wildlife conservation. It would have been an abject repudiation of the win-win rhetoric and therefore generated a lot of attention, and with a lengthy shelf life. Although it may have qualified as an aggressive tactic, such a press release wouldn't have put the Service at high risk of backlash if she'd issued it at the tail end of the Clinton Administration. At that stage she'd have been a lame duck in a backwater of the political pond.

Newly elected presidents have some big fish to fry. They don't worry much about the lame ducks at Interior; they can't do much about them anyway. But the lame duck can deliver one last public message before taking a bow and heading for the door. We see it happen occasionally, yet not enough in my opinion. Lame ducks are usually too concerned about staying in or near the revolving door between high-level public and private-sector posts.

Yet until they walk out the door that last time, lame ducks have a lot of free press available to them, especially when they use it for a controversy. After that the opportunities melt like a snowflake on a stove pipe.

Jamie Clark went out quickly and quietly to the relative obscurity of a vice-presidential post with the nonprofit Defenders of Wildlife, where she eventually became the president and CEO. While Clark occasionally popped up in the esoteric environmental news, she never made a splash in the national press again. (If you're Joe Public, have you ever even heard of her?)

Alas, the directorate briefings turned out to be somewhat of a sideshow. I'd been hired for big-picture thinking, but the big picture turned out to be more than the leadership at headquarters could handle. After the early forays into the directorate, ecological economics was fenced out, and my policy work was gradually ratcheted down to the narrowest of issues.

For awhile, though, and thanks to the charisma and integrity of Rick Coleman, at least the morale of Refuge System staff was outstanding. All-hands meetings were well-attended, animated, and productive. Staff went back to their offices refreshed and purposeful. I wasn't aware of a single person who didn't respect and admire Coleman.

Shockingly, Coleman returned to his office one day to find a blue envelope. Federal employees know the one I'm talking about. In big bold letters the words are, "To be opened only by _____." In this case the envelope was to be opened only by Coleman, who was thusly informed of his impending transfer to the regional office in Portland, Oregon, just about as far from headquarters as one may physically be placed, short of Alaska or Hawaii. From then on he served in various capacities for Region 1 (Pacific Northwest) and later Region 6 (Northern Plains and Rockies). It was nothing to scoff at, career-wise, but nothing like his talents and performance warranted, either.

Unfortunately, then, Rick Coleman won't be central to the rest of this story. I would only add that in 2010, at the annual conference of the National Council for Science and the Environment, I heard an eloquent speech by Herman Daly (the father of steady-state economics who passed away in 2022). Daly was giving his acceptance speech for the Lifetime Achievement Award, and he graciously remarked, "Blessed are they who encourage others." I instantly thought of Coleman, even though I hadn't seen him in over ten years, and I lamented the fact that none of his replacements could be thought of in the same light.

The news of Rick Coleman's forced relocation stunned our headquarters staff. What could he have possibly done to warrant such a sudden, life-changing order? Most staffers assumed we were witnessing an unscrupulous power grab by someone in the Washington Office. But by whom? Jamie Clark? Dan Crasche? Both? Someone above both?

4

NON-PRIVY PRESIDENTS

When I signed on with the Fish and Wildlife Service, I envisioned our work on the topic of economic growth moving up from the Director to the next one in the food chain—the Secretary of the Interior—and so on. "And so on" reveals the potential of this strategy, for the next one up the food chain from the Secretary of the Interior is the President of the United States.

So now imagine you're a fly on the wall of the Cabinet Room at the White House, most likely a White House with a smarter, more open-minded president than some of recent memory, along with a balanced cabinet of specialists. You're witnessing the following discussion, held at a weekly briefing on domestic policy. You hear the words, and you might even imagine the intonations of your favorite candidate:

President: Good morning. Our focus this week is the economy. As you know, the second quarter report on GDP was *not* what we'd hoped for. The economy grew only an eighth of a point. That amounts to a growth rate around half a percent for the year, which would be one of the lowest rates in American history. So I really need all the thinking caps on tightly today. The question is: What can we do to stimulate the economy? What's the biggest problem? Is it consumer confidence? Is it some barrier to productivity? Is it a lack of opportunity in particular sectors? Or is it all of the above, and then some? I need your thoughts on this, and for now, please, nothing is off the table. Let's start with Commerce. James?

Secretary of Commerce: Well, Mr. President, consumer confidence is tepid, but our research indicates that's not the problem. The attitude of the consumer seems to be, "Build it and we will come." And for a lot of families I think the reality is, "Build it and we can *afford* to come," because wages are on par with inflation. So consumers are not the problem; instead, the challenge seems to be squarely on the supply side, but we don't think there's a silver bullet there either. We can help increase productivity through our research and development budgets, but we can only make a marginal difference in the pace of technological progress. I think what we really need at this time is a programmatic, comprehensive approach, similar to the Big Push of the 1950s. So, Mr. President, with your permission, I would like to appoint a blue-ribbon commission to scrutinize the tax code and some of the regulatory policies that affect the flow of capital, and to develop a report with recommendations. I'd like to call it the Fiscal Policy for Growth Commission.

President: The "FPGC" then? It does have an official ring to it. [The driest of chuckles around the room.] Your assessment resonates with me, too. I'd say it warrants further consideration. But let's hear some other ideas while we're all here today. Janis? I'd be interested in your thoughts. In the energy sector I hear a lot about solar futures, for example, but so far the gains seem slower than expected. Am I missing something?

Secretary of Energy: Thank you, Mr. President. Yes, agonizingly slow. To be honest, the most recent research has not been positive. The basic physics of photovoltaics haven't allowed for a wholesale shift to solar cells. Similarly, the economies of scale have been surprisingly limited with solar arrays and distribution systems. My honest assessment is that, purely for purposes of GDP growth in the next few years, we would need to re-affirm our commitment to fossil fuels: liquid, gas, coal… a sort of fossil-fueled Big Push. For GDP this year, I think the single biggest issue is our ability to import crude oil from the Canadian provinces. For example—and I don't mean to point fingers—but our oil imports from Alberta are hampered by the emissions regulations of the EPA. You may recall; under the previous Administration they extended these regulations to cover imports as well as domestic production.

President: That's OK, I don't mean to point fingers either. [Looser laughing around the table.] Nevertheless, I think we should hear the concerns *of* the EPA. We want economic growth, for sure, but not at the expense of our clean air and water. What do you say, Helen?

EPA Administrator: Well, Mr. President, we have always taken the position at EPA that there is no conflict between growing the economy and protecting the environment, but reconciling these two goals has been a daunting challenge. It seems that, for every environmental problem we solve with new technology, another one or two arises from other new tech. On the specific issue of the Alberta tar sands, we may be able to import the product [crude oil from tar sands] with minimal damage to water supplies along the pipelines in the states, but the environmental impact of the tar sand operations in Alberta is extreme by any standard. The international agreements on greenhouse gas emissions are jeopardized by our trade in tar-sand oil, too. Frankly I'm a little dismayed to hear the Energy Secretary's report. I just don't know where we go from here, to reconcile GDP growth with environmental protection.

President: I hear that. We've got to figure out a way to grow the economy without a dependence on tar sands, of all things. I've seen the satellite imagery from Alberta, and it seems to me that would be a big step backwards. Maybe we need to look in other places for economic capacity. Energy is crucial of course but it seems to me there are other possibilities in terms of how we *use* energy to grow the economy. Any thoughts? Anyone else is welcome to chime in. Again, nothing is off the table.

[Some seconds of uncomfortable silence. Then a clearing of a throat...]

Secretary of the Interior: Well, Mr. President, and given the segue, I feel obliged to say something here... [a pause and a straightening of posture]... Mr. President, what I have to say is that, for us at Interior, in recent years especially, GDP growth has posed as many challenges as the lack of it has. Every month, every week it seems, this has become more of a topic of discussion among my senior advisors and agency leadership. They like to remind me that, at the end of the day, GDP growth simply means increasing production and consumption of goods and services, with the inevitable pressures on our natural resources and our environment. My Fish and Wildlife Director calls it the "800-Pound Gorilla," because they have a long history there of avoiding the topic, even though they all seem to be aware of it. They're afraid it will cause a congressional backlash against them, and they prohibit their employees from even talking about it. Yet I've been forced to think about it for some time now, and frankly I see it throughout my travels, including the northern Rockies with Alberta next door. So Helen's comments resonate with me. I can't say that economic growth shouldn't continue to be the primary domestic policy goal—that's not our job at Interior—but I think it is my job in this venue to question whether we can continue to reconcile growth with environmental protection. In fact, maybe we never really *did* reconcile the two. We have of course developed some "green" technologies, but we've also boxed ourselves into more of a corner, decade by decade, in terms of our remaining resources and the stability of our environment. Climate change is the most ominous challenge, but long before climate change we were besieged with a long list of daunting problems like water shortages, soil erosion, and biodiversity loss. None of these problems has gone away; in fact, each one has intensified in lock-step with GDP. These environmental issues are linked with social problems such as the threats to the cultural identity of our rural communities. Let me just add that the easiest way to understand the conflict between growth and the environment is with the issue of endangered species. The causes of species decline are like a who's who of the American economy, and there is a well-developed scientific literature describing the conflict between economic growth and biodiversity conservation. These other species are like the canaries in the coalmine of the American economy. I am concerned that the conflict between economic growth and environmental protection, in other words, is quickly becoming a conflict between economic growth and economic *sustainability*, and even national security and international stability.

[Silence for longer than usual.]

President: You know what, Roger? I really appreciate your honesty and courage. You felt "obliged to say something"—I think that's how you put it—and you sure did say it! [Relief and laughter around the table.] I too have been hearing more about the challenges posed by economic growth. I am still trying to digest it all. It could very well be that those calling for a "steady state economy," or even those in Europe calling for "degrowth," will be proven by history to be all the wiser. It's definitely a new way of looking at things for me. I'm afraid my economics training was pretty standard, so I'll need more input from Interior and EPA, and I welcome it. Thank you all. I will consider the earlier recommendation of a blue-ribbon committee, too. It would at least be good to know the options. Meanwhile, I'll also be consulting with the Council of Economic Advisors and the Federal Reserve about the role of monetary policy in all this. It could very well be the case that we may need to live with a lower growth rate in the 21st century than the one we enjoyed in the 20th; I want to hear their thoughts on it, too. We'd certainly have some work to do in communicating this to the American public, but perhaps it's time we start trying to do so. If my history isn't too far off, President Carter alluded to this about 50 years ago. The time wasn't ripe—the press turned it into the "malaise speech"—but maybe the time has come. Maybe they should have called it the "brave speech." Stay tuned and let's resume this discussion soon.

The Cabinet-level discussion would not, on its own, a steady state economy make. In fact, limited to the President and Cabinet, the discussion wouldn't even go very far toward raising public awareness of the trade-off between economic growth and wildlife conservation. That said, can you imagine a steady state economy ever becoming reality *without* such preliminary discussions among presidents and appointees? Of course not. The President doesn't just appear one day and say, "Cabinet, let's establish a steady state economy." Preliminary discussions are the first essential steps toward the reforming of fiscal and monetary policy, away from rapid GDP growth and toward the steady state economy.

At this point in history, however, even a preliminary discussion is almost impossible to fathom. First, the members of the Cabinet, or *one* of them at least, has to be aware of the threats posed by economic growth. They need more than just a dim awareness, too; they need a significant amount of familiarity with the concepts and the evidence. Enough to speak authoritatively and persuasively among a group of extremely intelligent, articulate, and driven high-level officials. They also need a shot of courage—as with our hypothetical Interior secretary—to raise such an issue in prime time with the president. But that should be a secondary concern because anyone who has made it to the Cabinet level is no wilting wallflower. The key thing is knowledge and awareness, which naturally complements the courage—blatant or latent—of a high-level advisor.

Therein lies the relevance of FWS, other Interior agencies, the EPA, and similarly enlightened segments and individuals in the federal government. Why put the onus on them? It's a fair and important question.

Consider what the hypothetical Interior secretary, "Roger," had to say to the president: "The easiest way to understand the conflict between economic growth and environmental protection is with the issue of endangered species." He explained, "The causes of species decline are like a who's who of the American economy, and there is a well-developed scientific literature describing the conflict between economic growth and biodiversity conservation." He pointed out that "These other species are like the canaries in the coal mine of the American economy."

What other members of the president's cabinet would be as familiar and articulate with the conflict between economic growth and biodiversity conservation? Surely none, because no others would be in frequent and detailed contact with the FWS, the primary administrator of the Endangered Species Act and the primary employer of the wildlife biologists familiar with the causes of endangerment.

Our Secretary of the Interior was bigger-thinking than most. He didn't stop at the conflict between economic growth and biodiversity conservation, or even at the conflict between growth and environmental protection at large. No, Roger insisted that "the conflict between economic growth and environmental protection… is quickly becoming a conflict between economic growth and economic sustainability, and even national security and international stability."

It was a bold, big-thinking statement that ventured beyond Interior's traditional stovepipe and into the territories of Agriculture, Commerce, Housing, Transportation, and even Defense and State. In other words, the Secretary of the Interior engaged most of the President's cabinet directly with the 800-Pound Gorilla. It was a strategic statement as well, because without engaging these other departments, there would be little hope of the policy reforms required for a steady state economy. Even more importantly, the President needed the support of the full Cabinet, or most of it at least, to run with such a paradigm shift. He was willing to lead—he saw himself as an agent of change—but not without a ready column of heavy hitters covering his back.

It wasn't an easy fit for Roger, but it wasn't beyond the pale either. He had thought it out and realized that, once he got past the immediate conflict between economic growth and biodiversity conservation (which took some special expertise), the rest of the argument was fairly a matter of common sense. To wit: 1) No environment, no economy. 2). No economy, no national security. 3) No national security, no international stability. It's a simple matter of connecting the dots.

That was the vision, at least.

Was the vision too big? It certainly was for Dan Crasche and a long list of FWS appointees and bureaucrats. Their approach, instead, was to *undermine and block* any efforts to apprise higher-level officials of the conflict between growth and the environment. They were more concerned with their particular appointments and the paths of least resistance.

Only time will tell if the vision was too big for the 21st century FWS, or just the right size for success. At least one member of the Service's inner circle, Greg Siekaniec, acknowledged on several occasions that I wasn't wrong with my steady-state vision. Starting in 2000 he assured me I was only "ahead of the times."[16] With regard to when we could get serious about the 800-Pound Gorilla, he surmised, "maybe in 15 years," but as with most bureaucrats, his

---

[16] Greg Siekaniec was my immediate supervisor when I was hired in 1999. In a matter of years he became the Chief of the National Wildlife Refuge System, but then transferred

"maybe" meant nothing and the timeline was way off. I spent almost 20 years with FWS and the breakthrough moments were always superseded by backward steps, most notably more gag orders.

Whatever timeline the bureaucrat estimates, you should double it, and triple it for appointees. So perhaps instead of being 15-20 years ahead of the times, I was 30 or 40 years ahead. By 2030 or 2040, then, we should expect our federal employees to help raise awareness of the trade-off between economic growth and wildlife conservation.

I hope *Gag-Ordered No More* persists in print for a good 20 years, long enough to spur some action in the civil service, because honestly and disturbingly, I see no other effort stirring in the civil service to raise public awareness of the 800-Pound Gorilla. And efforts like this, on topics this big, take time to incubate. But in 20 years the limits to growth and the conflict between economic growth and environmental protection will be exceedingly obvious to a much larger portion of the wildlife profession, the civil service, the general public, and politicians. By then, federal employees may appear foolish if they *don't* talk about the problems caused by economic growth.

The problem is, 20 years from now, after so many decades of industrial-strength, lightning-speed, computerized, officially sanctioned, politically polished, policy-greased, global economic growth, the planetary ecosystem may be irrevocably unravelling toward a new, devastating reality. To put it in more economically relevant terms, the foundation of the global economy may be crumbling beneath our feet. Call it alarmist rhetoric if you're so inclined, but mark these words: Nations will be aggressively looking for more resources, more land, more room to live, far more aggressively than they are today.

More room to live… what did they call that once upon a time? Oh yes, "Lebensraum."

But don't worry. According to FWS leadership, "there is no conflict between growing the economy and protecting the environment." And of course, FWS only operates pursuant to "sound science."

Feel better?

---

out of the government, to Ducks Unlimited Canada. In 2016 he returned to the Fish and Wildlife Service as a regional director.

5

ECOLOGICAL INTEGRITY

vs.

THE 800-POUND GORILLA

The first task I faced upon arriving at Refuge System headquarters was developing a new and controversial Refuge System policy made necessary by the National Wildlife Refuge Improvement Act of 1997. The Refuge Improvement Act had a clause requiring the Secretary of the Interior (via the Fish and Wildlife Service) to "maintain the biological integrity, diversity, and environmental health" of the Refuge System. I brought in the phrase "ecological integrity" to summarize the 20-syllable "biological integrity, diversity, and environmental health."

Developing the ecological integrity policy was a natural fit. While pursuing a master's degree at the University of Washington, I'd gotten conversant with the precedent-setting research of James Karr and colleagues such as Paul Angermeier on the ecological integrity of aquatic systems. I saw their research as highly relevant to land management decision-making in literally every type of ecosystem. Shortly after the master's program, down on the San Carlos Apache Reservation, I used the ecological integrity concept to push back against the aggressive timber-harvesting proposals of the BIA's forestry program.

Ecological integrity became a central concept in my Ph.D. program as well because endangered species indicate the compromising of natural conditions.

By the time I signed on with FWS, then, I had been exploring and applying the concept of ecological integrity for 15 years. I was shocked to find that the concept was new and puzzling to the team of regional refuge biologists already assembled at the policy table. This gave me the first inkling that the FWS might not be as full of expertise as I'd assumed.

Unfortunately, by the time I arrived there was plenty of policy turf already staked out, which made for tough sledding during my first year at headquarters. Splintered groups of the regional biologists had drafted competing versions of the policy, none of which were workable. One of the versions even interpreted the Refuge Improvement Act as a call for "administrative integrity." (It's possible that version was intended as an inside joke, in which case it would have been a good one!)

Working as fast as I could, before the existing versions could take further root, I drafted a new ecological integrity policy from scratch. It took most of my first month at headquarters, and it kicked off not only the Refuge System ecological integrity policy but the formal introduction of the 800-Pound Gorilla to the FWS. Here's how:

"Integrity" in this case meant whole, natural, unadulterated conditions. That much can be gleaned from Webster's dictionary.

Biological integrity, then, meant natural biological conditions. For example, biological integrity entails native species coexisting in fairly natural proportions. Lots of bison and prairie dogs coexisting with some wolves and black-footed ferrets; that's a sign of biological integrity on the Great Plains. Roundup-Ready soybean fields interspersed with feedlots, not so much.

Environmental health was essentially the equivalent of biological integrity, except in the physical, chemical sense. Clean air and clean water are obvious examples of environmental health, but the term also includes less obvious background conditions like the natural climate, wildfire, and hydrological cycles.

Putting the two components together—biological integrity and environmental health—simply added up to "natural conditions," period. So why not use a shorter phrase to summarize the 16 syllables? Fortunately "ecological integrity" was right there for the taking, with an award-winning tradition already in academia as well as some usage in the U.S. Park Service and the Canadian government.

Not that any of this came easily to the team I stepped in front of. I was the new kid on the block and the older Toms and Freds and Waynes didn't like their turf being plowed up and reseeded. One fellow from a regional office quit the team and was never heard from again! Team meetings were notorious for heated exchanges that were overheard in the hallways. One creative, fun-loving fellow with a nearby office even took the time to compose a ballad, "The Charge of the Ecological Integrity Team, with Apologies to Lord Alfred Tennyson."

Weird Al Yankovic would have been proud.

After the dust settled a bit, and notions of "administrative integrity" were put out to pasture, the ecological integrity clause didn't seem so daunting after all. We were simply called by the Refuge Improvement Act to keep things natural on the Refuge System, although we had to balance that with other aspects of the act as well as other laws and policies governing the Refuge System. It was all about a healthy balance. We couldn't just turn the keys back over to Mother Nature and hope for the best, but we couldn't turn the Refuge System into a collection of zoological facilities, either. We had to conserve and manage migratory birds, endangered species, and other "trust species" under natural conditions, or at least as natural as feasible. How's that for common sense?

On the other hand, this approach left us with the million-dollar question: What *were* "natural conditions?" That's the question that led us straight to the 800-Pound Gorilla. Let's see how that happened, and how it led to the first (presumably) gag order on economic growth in the history of FWS, and perhaps in the history of the federal government.

The very concept of naturalness—and integrity—is meaningless without some starting point or frame of reference. But then, for ecological purposes, you can't simply take a snapshot in time and call that natural, either. You can't say, "In 1868 General Sheridan counted 400 buffalo and 3 wolves on the Washita Plain" and assume the benchmark for ecological integrity on the Washita Plain is 400 bison and 3 wolves. You need to consider a lengthy and relevant period of time. You need a chronology with meaningful starting and ending points. You need, in other words, a frame of reference for natural conditions, in particular a chronological frame of reference.

So the million-dollar question quickly became, "What is the *frame of reference* for natural conditions?" Of course, there is no absolutely correct answer. First of all, there isn't ample information about how natural things were at any given time in the distant past. What if a rare disease had knocked back the prairie dog population for a few decades?

Second, the whole exercise is riddled with subjectivity and philosophical challenges; was that "rare" disease really so unnatural itself?

And third, why would any of it matter if it was entirely out of touch with the public? There would have to be at least a shred of common sense and taxpayer appreciation for the chronological frame of reference to pass the public review stage.

This was exactly the type of "complex environmental problem" requiring "innovative and imaginative ways" my position description had called for. It required integrating the natural and social sciences to solve a thorny policy development problem with long-term implications for federal land management.

Hearkening back to courses in biogeography, evolutionary ecology, and climate change, I recalled a stint with the Council of Athabascan Tribal Governments in the Yukon Flats of Alaska, where I was hired to do a feasibility study for introducing wood bison. Part of that job was interviewing tribal elders to determine if there was any oral history of wood bison in the Flats. The question, in other words, had to do with the ecological integrity of putting wood bison there, and the tribal members "got it" without fail. If the wood bison were there before the white man came in and reshuffled the ecological deck, then they belonged there again, because that would be ecological integrity. So, they searched their memory banks and we talked, and I also did some homework on the fossil and archeological records.

It was more than a decade of education and experience, then, that led me to hone in on the year 800 CE as the beginning point for the frame of reference. Remember, you had to set *some* date, or else be accused of having a squishy policy. It was a thankless challenge, because any date you picked would expose you to critique or even ridicule. But I made my case for 800 CE as follows: You couldn't go way, *way* back in time—dinosaurs were irrelevant to the conversation. Yet you had to go back far enough to accommodate the cycles of nature, especially climate oscillations such as the warming El Niño and the cooling La Niña.

Except for the rarest of exceptions, climate change wasn't on the mind of the FWS yet, either. And to be fair, it was even further from the minds of other federal agencies. Yet the benchmark of 800 CE had something to offer on that front as well, because going back to 800 CE thoroughly encompassed the "Medieval Warm Period" (circa 950–1250 CE), which was followed by a moderate climate for almost a century. Then came the "Little Ice Age" (circa 1350–1850 CE). So, by going back to the year 800, we would be encompassing over a thousand years of climatological, evolutionary, and biogeographic pathways and processes.

Now we were onto something eminently reasonable. If you were managing the habitats of the Buenos Aires National Wildlife Refuge in Arizona, for example, your homework may have told you that much of the area had been Sonoran desert for hundreds of years prior to the cattle baron days, and may have hosted some lush desert grasslands, with stands of pinyon-juniper at times. Managing for these types of habitats would be "fair game" pursuant to the ecological integrity policy. Excavating a 50,000-acre lake or planting a stand of loblolly pine would not be, because never in the chronological frame of reference was there anything remotely resembling either of those ecosystems.

But what about the other end—the near end—of the frame of reference? The whole idea was to use the past, when conditions were more natural, so it wouldn't make much sense to include the year 1999, would it? Some would argue that, by the end of the 20th century, or even by mid-century, *nothing* in the world was really natural anymore. So how far back did we have to go to "encounter" the last of the natural conditions?

Just as the year 800 CE appears naturally enough (so to speak) as a starting point for the frame of reference, the year 1800 comes into focus as a logical ending point. For anyone with a rough understanding of American history, that should already resonate. But now your challenge, as a policy writer, is to explain *why*, and to explain it in relatively precise, technical, and resonating terms. Why would 1800 serve as a logical, objective ending point of natural conditions?

Drumroll, please, for the 800-Pound Gorilla.

I and the ecological integrity team would proffer the following: The American economy was in the midst of an extremely rapid expansion circa 1800, due to the industrial revolution, and it was starting to put its stamp across the landscapes of the United States, at least over most of the contiguous 48 states. Ecological and environmental conditions rapidly became far less natural. New York City already had 60,000 people packed into less than a thousand acres.[17] Coal-fired pollution became a major problem in the bigger cities and their airsheds. Throughout the coming decades the countryside would be dramatically transformed by the plow and the steam engine. Wildlife populations were thrown out of balance by market hunting and trapping. Logging and mining commenced in earnest, and ranchers fenced the West. You pretty much had to go back to 1800, when Lewis and Clark were still planning their journey, to find natural conditions through much of the country.

Before continuing our exploration of natural conditions and ecological integrity we have to acknowledge—and observe a moment of silence for—the Native Americans, past and present. Seriously, let's do that, putting the

---

[17] See "Demographia" website, derived from historic U.S. Census Bureau data, http://www.demographia.com/db-nyuza1800.htm .

book down for a moment and paying our respect, for so much was lost to them. For that matter, so many *of* them were lost.

For the Native Americans—or "American Indians" as many themselves prefer—by 1800 "natural conditions" had already deteriorated for centuries, going back at least to 1492, as smallpox had decimated their settlements, cultures, and economies.

This raises the issue that the collective Native American economy had been growing throughout the Holocene (the period of time since the end of the Pleistocene ice ages which ended approximately 12,000 years ago), and that *it*—the Native American economy—was itself having a growing effect on wildlife and ecosystems. This obvious fact was cited by some to challenge our designation of 1800 as the endpoint of natural conditions, and to argue that the endpoint should have been earlier, before the impact of Native Americans became so large. In a few cases there was a thinly veiled undertone that it was prejudicial to "blame" the European immigrants for ending the era of ecological integrity. Nonsense. The salient point is that, regardless of whose economy was growing (Native Americans' or others'), or how it was being fueled, it was the dramatic *jump in the rate of growth* that could be objectively used as an endpoint of natural conditions.

The jump in the rate was not normal; it was unnatural. Something was "new under the sun," as the historian J.R. McNeill would put it.[18] W.W. Rostow, the great compiler of economic growth theory, called this jump in the rate of growth the American "take-off." The jump was statistically identifiable and distinctive, which is why it works so well to mark the endpoint of natural conditions.[19]

In my opinion, "blame" is hardly a relevant issue here. The relevant issue is ecological macroeconomics. It's a fact of ecological macroeconomics that the human economy grows at the competitive exclusion of non-human species in the aggregate. It's a closely related fact of ecological macroeconomics that there is a conflict between economic growth and ecological integrity. It follows that an episode of very fast growth stands out from the long, slow, evolutionary rates of growth of pre-industrial times. Finally, it's a perfectly logical sequitur—and a policy-relevant one—that 1800 be cited as an ending point for ecological integrity.

---

[18] McNeill, J.R. 2000. *Something New under the Sun: An Environmental History of the Twentieth-Century World*. W.W. Norton, New York. 421pp.

[19] See Czech, B. 2005. A chronological frame of reference for ecological integrity and natural conditions. *Natural Resources Journal* 44(4):1113-1136.

If we were able to watch a movie with time-lapse photography of the human economy growing over the area that is now the United States, we'd see the economy growing very slowly for much of the Holocene. Then the industrial revolution occurs and the economy skyrockets, and for a fairly long time, because there are still immense stocks of natural resources available over the American landscape. These stocks take the shape of forests, woodlands, grasslands, lakes, rivers, and underground deposits of minerals, ores, oil, and gas. Wetlands and deserts, too, provide valuable resources. Furthermore, all types of land provide space—an overlooked resource—for economic expansion.

But of course all these landscapes were originally, naturally occupied by wildlife, and the "natural resources" had simply comprised wildlife habitats prior to their liquidation and conversion into producer and consumer goods and services.

The ecological science behind the frame of reference was as sound as the law of gravity, so we provided a thumbnail sketch of it in the draft ecological integrity policy. To my knowledge, this was the first instance of the phrase "economic growth" appearing in any FWS policy, and it was certainly the first instance, perhaps in the history of the federal government at large, in which "economic growth" was formally revealed as problematic in some way. Frankly, I was proud of it. If I'd had my druthers, I would have elaborated further on the frame of reference and in particular the role of industrial-speed economic growth in ushering away the era of ecological integrity. But we had the basics in the draft policy that went out for public review, and that was infinitely better than nothing.

The draft policy did well under public scrutiny, too. There were very few public comments against it, and virtually none against the aspects noted above. The few negative comments came almost exclusively from a handful of politicians who could be counted on to oppose virtually anything coming out of the FWS. The best example was Don Young of Alaska, the blowhard who bullied his way around his little political fishbowl. Young argued that, since "ecological integrity" was not in the Refuge Improvement Act, we could not introduce the term into a Refuge System policy.

How absurd was Young's critique. Of course we could introduce the term ecological integrity in a policy. As with most federal agencies, we introduced terms in policies all the time, as the state of the art advanced. We were about to do so here, with verve and nuance, capitalizing on the rigorous and award-winning literature on the topic of ecological integrity.

But the joke was on me and the rest of the ecological integrity team when the new chief of the Refuge System—Tim Dirth—caved in and yanked the term "ecological integrity" from the policy our team had spent two years developing.

If you don't think the words matter, ask the politicians that steer public opinion with slogans like "Change We Can Believe In" or "No Child Left Behind" or "Make America Great Again." The name of a key policy ought to resonate like a slogan, especially if it can easily do so without distorting the content. In this case, it's not like we were putting lipstick on a pig: "ecological integrity" truly integrates the concepts of biological integrity, diversity, and environmental health. It packs a lot of nuance into a succinct and flowing phrase.

That's why "ecological integrity policy" was beginning to resonate in the conservation community before Dirth cursed it with the 23-syllable, non-flowing, bureaucratically bumbling "Biological Integrity, Diversity, and Environmental Health Policy." That inefficient mouthful (try it a few times) gave rise to the acronym "BIDEH," which has the phonetic properties of a sump pump. Refuge System regulars finally started calling it "601 FW 3," after its location in the FWS policy manual. Yes, even "601 FW 3" sounded better than "BIDEH."

It wouldn't matter so much if we were talking about the Vehicle Towing Policy or the Metric Conversion Policy (actual policies in the *Fish and Wildlife Manual*), but "601 FW 3" is the central pillar of Refuge System management philosophy! It's where the Refuge Improvement Act meets 21st century conservation biology. The content of it occupies thousands of conversations a year among Refuge System staff, other FWS personnel, and elsewhere on the conservation landscape. If each of these conversations were rife with the phrase "ecological integrity," the effect would be conducive to big-picture, nuanced, interdisciplinary thinking about conservation. Furthermore, "ecological integrity policy" would have sent a message that the tax-paid FWS had done its homework and was leading the way with state-of-the-art concepts.

I was confident of all that because I'd seen and heard the effect of the phrase "ecological integrity" in academia and government (at the nexus of tribal, federal, and state agencies). If you're the wildlife biologist on a land management planning team and you say, "Protecting that riparian area would be more conducive to the ecological integrity of the region," it carries a bigger, more holistic message than "Protecting that riparian area would be better for bluntnose shiners and riffle beetles."

Invoking "ecological integrity" makes people stop, think, and integrate the key issues in conservation. They think about the whole, not just the parts. They start to think more like Thoreau, who invoked the wisdom of his readers with, "A gun gives you the body, not the bird."[20]

This big-thinking effect had started to percolate at FWS, too. During the long, draft phase of the policy's development, the phrase "ecological integrity" was effective *in* the policy and in the title *of* the policy. The more people used it, the more they saw its utility in bringing together the biological and physical elements of naturalness, and of communicating the concept in nine syllables.

It's not that our original naming of the policy would have led to world peace and a cure for cancer, but it clearly would have made a difference in the mindset of Refuge System employees. Over time, these employees would be reaching millions of visitors; in the field, online, and through social media. It was, in fact, this difference in mindset that threatened the hook-and-bullet politics of Don Young. He wanted to cut the ecological integrity mindset off at the pass, and keep the Refuge System geared toward churning out ducks and geese. In his estimation, Thoreau's "bird" didn't matter to his constituents; it was all about the body (plus the guns and the shooting).

So Dirth's cave-in was bad enough, but he went so far as to prohibit me from even using the phrase "ecological integrity" in the context of the policy, even in *discussions in the hallway*! He made sure the lower chiefs were aware of this, and they saw to it that I complied. (A fellow by the name of Seaze, for example, was a real hallway monitor.) This was my introduction to the propensity of "chiefs" to censor, as well as the enthusiasm of some lower chiefs to enforce. The prohibition was for all intents and purposes a gag order, but Dirth issued it verbally and was, therefore, hardly accountable for it.

If I don't sound entirely respectful of Dirth herein, respect began to wane no later than this draconian gag order.

Meanwhile, Don Young also honed in on the frame of reference, which was where the 800-Pound Gorilla was identified for all to see. I feared the worst and, sure enough, Dirth ordered us to drop the frame of reference too. Maybe Don Young had something on Dirth, who'd spent much of his FWS career in Alaska. It made people wonder, because we didn't have to

---

[20] This saying is attributed to Henry David Thoreau. See for example yourdictionary.com.

kowtow to a lone congressional representative, especially when others had stated their support.

The team and I attempted to keep as much of the baby's head above water as possible while we incorporated the bathwater of Dirth's replacement language. I insisted on retaining at least some language on economic growth in the policy, as it was central to the whole concept of ecological integrity (or if you prefer, "biological integrity, diversity, and environmental health"). The team agreed, and I felt vindicated and appreciative that they had come to understand the 800-Pound Gorilla and the importance of exposing it. We even got a grudging acknowledgment from Dirth that, "Well, we can leave a *tiny bit* of it, but that's all." The problem was, we couldn't count on a tiny bit of Dirth's word.

The following week I was at a meeting out of town, and when I got back the policy was in surnaming (that is, making its final rounds for approval by the chain of command). I was shocked to find that *all references to economic growth were completely gone*. I felt betrayed, because I *was* betrayed—as was the team—and I got angry. I grabbed the surnaming package and went looking for Dirth, trying everything in my power to back it out of surnaming and reclaim the "tiny bit" he assured us would remain. Dirth was obstinate and, ultimately, he had the upper hand. He had pulled rank and deleted the language, and now he refused to budge.

It's not that Dirth had a technical disagreement with what we had written, either; quite the opposite. I knew this because, during the latter stages of the policy's development, I had a chance to brief Dirth on the relationship between economic growth and wildlife conservation. I gave him nearly the same presentation I'd given the directorate. It was a closed-door presentation exclusively for Dirth and a branch chief, Elizabeth Souheaver. Unlike the enthusiastic reaction of Jamie Clark, Dirth's dismissive reaction was, "Everybody knows there's a conflict between economic growth and wildlife conservation. It's just not our role to talk about it."

Dirth was known for a healthy ego, and never wanted to be second in thought. No doubt Dirth had a vague sense of the conflict between growth and conservation, as any career wildlife professional would have. Yet he'd never uttered a single word about the conflict, much less with any original insights. As the Chinese-American philosopher Yi-Fu Tuan observed: "People tend to suppress that which they cannot express."[21]

---

[21] Tuan, Y. 1977. *Space and Place: The Perspective of Experience*. University of Minnesota Press, Minneapolis. 235pp. See p. 6.

At least Dirth acknowledged the conflict between economic growth and wildlife conservation. However, his claim that "everybody knows there's a conflict" was ignorant and showed he hadn't been listening. I had summarized how mainstream, conventional economics had long ago lost its connection with the land and, for decades, had been advancing a theory of perpetual economic growth. (Most readers who took a business or economics course will sense what I'm talking about.) Perpetual growth theory was favored by Big-Money special interests and politicians in need of win-win rhetoric, so it survived in academia and had plenty of followers. That explained why the president of the National Wildlife Federation (who was an economist!) and virtually every card-carrying member of the American Economic Association denied such a conflict.

I had also noted that many who *did* see the conflict—including a lot of people in the wildlife profession—failed to say a single thing about it. Ironically enough, perhaps they were thinking, "Everybody knows there's a conflict." More typically, perhaps, they just couldn't be bothered, or frankly didn't have the fortitude to broach the topic.

For yet others, although they saw the conflict in the field, they didn't know *how* to talk about it in economic terms. They didn't feel comfortable in venues where economic policy was discussed, either.

Yet the biggest irony of all was the one I left out of the presentation, namely, that political appointees like Dan Crasche—Dirth's boss and buddy—had been out huckstering the public for years with "There is no conflict between economic growth and wildlife conservation." Now Crasche's right-hand man was telling me that we didn't need to be talking about the conflict between economic growth and wildlife conservation because "everybody knows there's a conflict."

The ironies never cease, but some are more ironic than others!

Not long before I briefed Dirth, I was invited to give a talk at Rennselaer Polytechnic Institute in Troy, New York. The talk was similar to the one I would give Dirth and Souheaver (and the one I'd given Clark). Afterward one of the professors, Carl McDaniel, was effusive with appreciation. Part of the effusiveness was just Carl, who became a long-time friend and colleague of sorts. But as he explained it, "You know, I always thought there was a conflict, but I didn't really know *how to express it.* I'd never seen anybody put all the pieces together like that. Now I really get it."

Most of the Refuge System chiefs, while forced to acknowledge the conflict, never really got it.

Part Two

UNDER DAMOCLES' SWORD

So, in the interests of survival, they trained themselves to be agreeing machines instead of thinking machines.

Kurt Vonnegut Jr., *Breakfast of Champions*

There are two kinds of idiots — those who don't take action because they have received a threat, and those who think they are taking action because they have issued a threat.

Paulo Coelho, *The Devil and Miss Prym*

6

THE BIBLE CLUB AND GAG-ORDER CREEP

It didn't take long for Tim Dirth to engender an "us vs. them" sociology in Refuge System headquarters by developing a select circle of after-work drinkers. Typically starting around 4:00, he'd lead them across Utah Street to The Willow, a local watering hole for bureaucrats and businesspeople, plus patrons from The Nature Conservancy and the National Science Foundation. Dirth's circle of drinkers came to be known as the "Bible Club."

While "Bible Club" was used in jest inside the club, outside the club it was used more cynically. The Bible Club quickly developed the traits of a privileged, exclusive clique with a well-defined doctrine. Whatever Dirth said was "bible" and clearly divined from Dan Crasche. If you were a lower chief, aspiring to higher-level chieftainship, the way to "get religion" was via spirits at the Willow. I can't think of a single branch chief or division chief in my chain of command, throughout the Dirth years, who wasn't in the Bible Club. Only the drinking location changed, when Refuge System headquarters moved to the Washington suburb of Falls Church, Virginia, in 2013.

One of the tenets of the Bible Club was that the 800-Pound Gorilla had to be ignored at all costs. All of the Bible Club drinkers—every single one—would come to oppose the idea that we should help raise awareness of the trade-off between economic growth and wildlife conservation. These opponents included those who at first resisted the temptation to capitulate.

So it came to be that, over the years and one at a time, exactly a dozen chiefs dangled the sword of Damocles over my career. Some of them hung it closer to the scalp than others, and at least two of them seemed to enjoy it, while others hung it less enthusiastically, ordered by Dirth to do so, who in turn was doing the bidding of Dan Crasche. A few of them were even reluctant to dangle the sword, and one, at least, attempted to have the whole approach reconsidered by Crasche, until he too eventually capitulated and (loosely) hung the sword.

Why didn't I make a bigger fuss early on? The best answer is a short story…

When I received the first gag order in 2001, I was flabbergasted and frustrated, and I confided in a close friend. She was a scientist at the National Research Council—a bastion of scientific integrity—and may have been even more flabbergasted than I. She was familiar with my research; we'd met at a conference where I'd spoken on the conflict between economic growth and biodiversity conservation.

My friend was so concerned about the suppression—at a supposedly science-driven agency—that she took the liberty of calling the ACLU to discuss potential legal action. She didn't mention FWS or name any individuals; she kept the discussion generic. She basically went on a legal scouting expedition and reported back to me.

Sixteen years later she reminded me of my response, which I'd long forgotten and would now deem naive. But evidently my reaction was somewhat touching to my friend, and it stuck in *her* memory. She reminded me that I'd told her I still had faith and hope in the leadership of FWS, even those who had issued the gag order. I told her I believed in the wildlife profession as a good, courageous, dignified crowd. It just *had* to be that way; we were doing God's work. Leadership would come around and recognize that ultimately wildlife conservation was all about stabilizing the size of the economy. They'd withdraw the gag orders and consult with me instead.

So I'd said "thank you," but I'd eschew the ACLU and wait for the dust to settle at FWS. Then I'd try my best to reason with the likes of Crasche, Dirth, and the branch chiefs they put above me.

And try I did, for years and years.

I hope FWS employees—past and present—will understand this well. I was no wild-eyed reactionary itching for a fight. Nothing was further from the truth. I *could have* gone to the ACLU, the Inspector General, the Government Accountability Office, the Office of Special Counsel, or the media. I did none of the above.[22] I knew from the start that raising awareness of the 800-Pound Gorilla was going to take patience, determination, strategy, and ultimately some luck with the chain of command. I had 17 years of patience and determination. I always had strategy, which evolved with the political times and environmental events.

But there was only one year of luck with the chain of command; the

---

[22] I finally filed a complaint with the Office of Special Counsel on the cusp of retirement in late 2017. I charged my Refuge System chain of command—several individuals in particular—with abuse of authority. The case was pending at the time of this writing.

year with Coleman at headquarters. Then Dirth arrived and commenced to adhering to the Peter Principle; he'd risen about as far as his competence could take him. Furthermore, he wouldn't want to be elsewhere. He probably realized he had become the quintessential, tax-paid, Refuge System 'tourist.' But during the first few years of his tenure, there was no way to know that he'd be running the Bible Club for decades.

Either way, I stubbornly held to the belief there'd be at least the *potential* for leadership with integrity in FWS. After all, at least a few of the chiefs were reluctant to hang the sword over me. Also, there were men and women of integrity in non-supervisory positions at Refuge System headquarters, plus lower chiefs in other chains of command, who disagreed with hiding the 800-Pound Gorilla. They weren't in the Bible Club, or not for long. They all found it distasteful and corrupting to be involved in suppressing the truth about economic growth and wildlife conservation. The problem was, none of them had had the benefit of an education in ecological economics, so they couldn't really talk shop thereon. Nor were any of them in strong positions politically. It was a bit like having sympathetic onlookers while getting beaten up by a gang on the street.

There seemed to be only one obvious thing to do in response to the Bible Club. Instead of going legally ballistic or taking my story to the Society of Environmental Journalists, I established a nonprofit organization, the Center for the Advancement of the Steady State Economy (CASSE). CASSE was chartered by the State of Virginia in 2003 and approved by the Internal Revenue Service as a 501(c)(3) educational organization in 2004. CASSE was—and still is—the only organization in the world explicitly devoted to advancing the steady state economy as a social and political goal.

I wouldn't have established CASSE if, a la Rick Coleman and the "original" Jamie Clark, the Service itself had developed the fortitude to tackle the 800-Pound Gorilla. The lack of fortitude was bad enough; the gag orders were over the top. I established CASSE as an outlet for the ecological economics that was off limits in the day job. CASSE would become one of the few silver linings in the sordid tale of a gagged career.

In CASSE's formative stages, I still had a strong social network at FWS. My first book, *Shoveling Fuel for a Runaway Train*, was making the rounds in FWS headquarters, which helped me identify prospective CASSE networkers. Several co-workers got me booked for public talks in and around the Washington, DC beltway. Federal employees from other agencies, especially the Environmental Protection Agency, Park Service, and Forest Service, took an active interest, as did program managers at the National Science Foundation and the National Research Council.

Meanwhile, I spent many a coffee break and lunch period canvassing various programs at FWS headquarters for biologists, economists, and planners with potential interests in ecological economics. Few had any in-depth knowledge about economic growth, but quite a few took substantial interest, especially in the Division of International Affairs, the Ecological Services Division, and the Division of Habitat Conservation. Two of the first CASSE board members—an open-minded economist and a migratory bird biologist—were from FWS headquarters.

A lesser few of the FWS staffers took a rapid, active interest in ecological economics, and in a few cases it was life-changing. One of them told me he experienced an "epiphany" while reading *Shoveling Fuel for a Runaway Train*. This was nothing theatrical—no leaping and speaking in tongues—but rather an intellectual paradigm shift. This fellow had graduated with a double major in economics and environmental studies from Penn. He'd taken several Wharton School business courses and he'd been, by his own estimation, a pro-growther with a materialistic lifestyle. His name was Rob Dietz.

Even before we talked, Dietz had begun to realize the agency life wasn't for him, but *Shoveling Fuel* helped him identify a post-government calling. He quit FWS and went into the nonprofit sector, and a year later I hired him as CASSE's first paid executive director. Dietz flourished and so did CASSE. Although we never quite procured the funding to staff CASSE substantially during Dietz's tenure, we developed a volunteer network that was the envy of many a nonprofit.

Another thing CASSE had going for it was the position on economic growth inherited from The Wildlife Society efforts described in Chapter 3. In addition to circulating this position among the professional, scientific societies such as the American Fisheries Society, Ecological Society of America, and Society for Conservation Biology, we made the position statement the central CASSE tactic in advancing the steady state economy. A long list of FWS employees signed the position, in person or online. These included numerous program directors outside the Refuge System, and even one former Director, Lynn Greenwalt, considered by many the most distinguished of FWS alumni.

Unfortunately, there just weren't enough allied Refuge System personnel in leadership roles to overcome the culture of secrecy and suppression wrought by Tim Dirth. Dirth was like a curse to CASSE, alternately hiding and overshadowing the CASSE position on economic growth. Meanwhile the sword of Damocles hanging over my career had a pronounced side effect, a phenomenon we might call "gag-order creep."

To illustrate the phenomenon, we start with the fact that "acting chiefs" and detailees were commonly brought in and tested for Bible Club fealty.[23] It was one of these detailees who made me aware of gag-order creep. She demonstrated how the gag order was creeping outward from my own office into the programs and agendas of others. It was like The Blob, squishing through the cracks below doors, sliming its way down the halls, lining the conference rooms, and enveloping the truth about economic growth, neutralizing and killing it. It became a monster akin to the "Kochtopus," the secretive Koch brothers' network that stalked the environmental sciences in government.[24] While the Kochs paid by the millions to suppress the truth, the chiefs of the Refuge System did it for beer!

The detailee in question—"Dee" no less—joined me for lunch one day. We talked a bit about the 800-pounder, and she was a classic example of why Dirth had been so wrong with his claim that "Everybody knows there's a conflict between economic growth and wildlife conservation." Dee, whose regular duty station was in Denver, knew essentially nothing about economic growth, ecological economics, or political economy. She acknowledged as much, but what little she *had* been taught adhered to the neoclassical theory of perpetual growth. She offered feebly, "There doesn't *have* to be a conflict, right?"

Although Dee's thoughts were tainted with neoclassical leanings, I assumed it wasn't a lost cause for her to explore the terrain of ecological economics. She seemed interested, at least. Unfortunately, our opportunity to talk had run its course during our lunch. We had to get back to the 'real' job.

But Dee would soon be flying back to Denver, and people tend to read on flights. So, upon returning to the office, as a close-out to our lunchtime conversation, I gave her a copy of *Supply Shock*, the 2013 book I'd spent nearly fourteen years (on and off) writing. *Supply Shock* is the 'whole enchilada'

---

[23] A detailee is a person with a temporary assignment, usually away from their home duty station. In Refuge System headquarters, we continually hosted detailees from all over the country. In the vast majority of cases these detailees were FWS employees. For many years a disproportionate number of these detailees were from duty stations in Alaska, where Tim Dirth's inner circle was particularly well-developed.

[24] The Kochtopus was especially aggressive against climate science. See https://www.campaigncc.org/climate_change/sceptics/funders

about limits to growth and the alternative of a steady state economy, written as a hybrid trade/textbook, along the lines of a Jared Diamond book (*Collapse*, for example). It had the imprimatur of Herman Daly, William Rees, and Lynn Greenwalt, among others.

I assumed Dee would find the book interesting to peruse, at least, during her return trip. I hoped her perusal would generate enough additional interest to result in a full reading. She thanked me for the book and we went back to our desks; hers in the chief's office and mine among the cubicles.

Much to my surprise, Dee appeared at my cubicle a scant minute later and said, "You know, considering all the circumstances, I don't feel comfortable taking this book. I better give it back to you."

Something was off about that. I've given away a lot of books over the years; possibly hundreds. That was the *first time* anyone had reacted that way. She was returning the book, without even a perusal, not because she wasn't at all interested in the topic, and not because she didn't find the topic relevant to the mission of the Fish and Wildlife Service, but rather as a sort of fealty to the branch chief.

That particular branch chief, Arun Lyze, was the last I'd endure. He had pre-programmed detailees to monitor my words and actions to ensure there were no violations of the gag order. As careful as I was to keep any discussion of the 800-Pound Gorilla out of the office and purely on personal time, the fact that I had a gag order—an intensively executed gag order—was enough to stifle any further *consideration* of the topic by other Service personnel, including detailees being groomed for leadership.

That's gag-order creep.

Could I be jumping to conclusions? Is it possible, for example, that Dee simply had too much luggage to carry? Well, purple Martians are possible, but Dee didn't say, "I have too much luggage." She said, "I *don't feel comfortable* taking this book. I *better* give it back to you." I'll grant her this much: It's *damned* uncomfortable in gag-order country.

A couple of months later, essentially the same thing happened—for the second time in my 16 years (at the time) as a book author. Now it was obvious this was no coincidence. Another acting branch chief, Peter, refused a copy of *Supply Shock*, this time instantaneously upon the offer. This was a fellow I'd become acquainted with 25 years prior, while serving as Recreation and Wildlife Director for the San Carlos Apache Tribe. (At the time, he was an up-and-coming biologist overseeing a wildlife forensics program in Oregon.)

I thought of him as one of the more intellectual Service employees, and I knew he was loosely aware of my interdisciplinary scholarship.

But no, the dark ages had come to FWS headquarters. From Crasche to Dirth to Lyze, out through the acting chiefs and detailees, the gag orders crept and the proverbial burning of books spread like a creeping grass fire. The effect was precisely the same as with literal book-burning: the "canceling" of the topic from the eyes, ears, and minds of the people.

Now, European nobility from the 14th century were expected to burn books at times. They were, after all, tyrants from the dark ages. But here we were in the 21st century, at the headquarters of a federal agency where "sound science" supposedly ruled, administered in the context of a professional, civil service in the world's shining democracy. The steady state economy should have been to perpetual growth rhetoric what the Enlightenment was to Ptolemaic astronomy.

Instead we had highly advantaged, handsomely paid, and most importantly *tax-paid* appointees, chiefs, and kowtowing detailees suppressing the truth about what could properly be classified as the single most important topic affecting the mission of their agency.

I knew it was time to quit. I'd had enough of the gag orders, book burning, and dark ages. But it was them I was quitting, not me. They still hadn't beaten the topic out of me, and history teaches that it's only a matter of time before the books overcome the burning. Truthful books survive, Phoenix-like, the fires of suppression, and they hatch new ones that build upon the truth and reveal the folly of censorship.

7

THE "BOLD IDEAS FORUM"

GETS SCRUBBED FROM THE INTERNET

As late as July 3, 2016 I was having serious doubts about whether to continue with this book. The project was taking more of a toll on my morale than I thought it would. I knew it would be a downer, but I didn't think I had enough morale *left* to take an additional psychological hit. I was correct on the first account but wrong on the second. It turns out I still had some morale to lose.

Writing this book entailed frequent self-reminders and pondering of the 16 years of gag orders, reprimands, suspensions and humiliating treatment I experienced at the hands of Dan Crasche, Tim Dirth, and various pre-programmed chiefs named, for example, Souheaver, Schultz, Seaze, Pudert, Pock, and Lyze. If morale was a ten-story building, writing this book was like pushing the basement button in the elevator. I was forced to reminisce, descending one story for each chief who'd been programmed by Crasche and Dirth to keep the 800-Pound Gorilla in the corner and out of the FWS hallways. I almost gave up in the middle of Chapter 3.

Then I saw the Director's email with the subject line, "Be Bold for Independence Day." Of all the hypocrisies I've seen committed by politicians and political appointees, the periodic calls by Dan Crasche to "be bold" were the most glaring examples and, for me in particular, the most infuriating. I decided right then and there to gut it out and finish the book, come hell or high water.

Consider the following paragraph from the July 3 email. This paragraph came after Crasche challenged "Service employees and our partners to be bold for conservation."

I hope you take that to heart. The challenges we face demand no less—but I know you're up to the task. You should know that our leadership will back you to the hilt...even if it leaves us with a few more gray hairs.

I wondered especially about the phrase "back you to the hilt," including the subconscious text. Did Crasche have something in mind about the hilt of a knife in your back? I couldn't help but wonder, given the "Bold Ideas Forum" from a few years prior.

As they say, fool me once, shame on you; fool me twice, shame on me. I wasn't going to be fooled by Dan Crasche, Tim Dirth, or any of the Bible Club again. Instead of risking a response to Crasche's disingenuous exhortation, I doubled down on *Gag-Ordered No More*, beginning with the paragraphs you just read. Whereas in the following paragraphs, we'll revisit the so-called "Bold Ideas Forum" of 2011.

The Bold Ideas Forum was part of a broader Fish and Wildlife Service initiative called "Conserving the Future." Conserving the Future was supposedly an effort to develop a new vision for the Refuge System, with input from the ground up in the conservation community. Not that a new vision was needed; quite the contrary. We were only 16 years removed from the National Wildlife Refuge System Improvement Act, which was a rich and nuanced organic act for the Refuge System.[25] It was built to last. Furthermore, we were only a few years removed from the original visioning effort that stemmed *from* the Refuge Improvement Act, called "Fulfilling the Promise."

Ideally, an organic act is passed at the dawn of an agency's existence. It states the mission, lays out the overall philosophy, and establishes the general rules of the game. As far as organic acts go, the Refuge Improvement Act was late in coming but worth the wait. The first national wildlife refuge was established by Theodore Roosevelt in 1903, but good things—especially good legislation—can take a long time to come to fruition, and the Refuge Improvement Act was quite an example.

The Refuge Improvement Act was thorough and visionary. It provided a philosophical foundation for treating the collection of national wildlife refuges as truly a system, not a bunch of scattered fiefdoms. The overarching philosophy of the Refuge System was the "wildlife first principle," which was exactly as it sounded. On the Refuge System, wildlife comes first. Numerous activities can occur on refuges, and numerous management decisions must

---

[25] See Fischman 2002, 2003.

be made, but wildlife conservation always stays foremost in Refuge System affairs.

The wildlife first principle is what most distinguishes the Refuge System from the other major systems of federal lands. The National Forest System (managed by the U.S. Forest Service) and Bureau of Land Management (BLM) lands are managed pursuant to "multiple-use" missions, with some notable exceptions.[26] The National Park System (managed by the National Park Service), meanwhile, is managed pursuant to a challenging two-fold mission: to preserve natural ecosystems and concurrently provide for public visitation. Only the Refuge System is focused on wildlife conservation. It has, in essence, a single-purpose mission.

Where public uses are appropriate and compatible with refuge purposes and the mission of the Refuge System, those, too, may be managed for. Not all potentially compatible uses are weighted equally. The Refuge Improvement Act identified six that were automatically deemed appropriate across the Refuge System at large (although in some cases, at particular refuges, some of these uses are not allowed). These priority uses, the "Big Six," are: 1) hunting; 2) fishing; 3) wildlife observation; 4) wildlife photography; 5) environmental education; and 6) environmental interpretation.

Ecological integrity, compatibility, and the Big Six priority uses: These can be recognized as the triumvirate of Refuge System philosophy. If we went with a four-cornerstone model instead, then the fourth would be found in the phrase calling for the "conservation of the ecosystems of the United States." This progressive clause was closely related to the ecological integrity clause, because the best way to conserve natural biodiversity is simply to protect, in sufficient acreage, a representative cross-section of ecosystems.

Put in the crudest of terms, if we maintain the ecological integrity of enough forests, woodlands, grasslands, wetlands, and deserts, we will automatically be conserving the full collection of species in the country. We will be preventing these species from becoming imperiled and engaging the regulatory teeth of the Endangered Species Act. In the language of conservation

---

[26] While almost 90% of BLM lands are managed for multiple-use purposes, 35 million acres are designated under the National Landscape Conservation System, the mission of which is to "conserve, protect, and restore these nationally significant landscapes that have outstanding cultural, ecological, and scientific values for the benefit of current and future generations." These lands include national monuments, wilderness areas, national scenic areas, etc. The National Forest System also includes specially designated lands (most notably wilderness areas) protected from most of the multiple-use activities.

biology, the conservation of ecosystems is described as a "coarse filter" for biodiversity conservation.

So it came as no surprise that my next major policy-related assignment, after the ecological integrity policy, was to help sort out the priorities among Refuge System goals and objectives as affected by the Refuge Improvement Act. A team was chartered—the National Goals Team—and my role was to bring our formulation of goals and objectives in line with the ecological integrity policy and, more generally, with the principles of conservation biology.

It was a challenging assignment for the team, considering the numerous laws, policies, and histories behind the establishment of 550 refuges (the approximate number at the time).[27] It would be difficult enough to take one fairly simple and well-known species—mallards for example—and settle upon a population objective for the Refuge System, then step that down to hundreds of refuges across four major and numerous minor flyways. The next step, though, would be an order of magnitude more difficult. You'd have to convert the mallard population objectives to habitat objectives in terms of acreages devoted to breeding grounds (for northern refuges) and wintering grounds (primarily for southern refuges). Then you'd have to figure out the requirements for supporting mallards along their migratory routes to the breeding grounds in spring and to the wintering grounds in fall. "Duck energy days" (or "energy-use days") is the currency used for that type of exercise.

None of this can be done in a vacuum. You have to coordinate with each of the other "stakeholders," most notably the state governments corresponding with the migratory routes, but also the other federal natural resource agencies, the tribes, private land trusts, and county governments—plus the Canadian, Mexican, and other Western Hemisphere governments. Each of their management priorities will affect the populations of migratory species on refuges. And of course those priorities change over time, and so do habitat conditions on the ground, plus other population variables such as predation, disease, and invasive species.

Multiply that difficulty by, say, a thousand species of fish and wildlife!

But wait, the challenges are far from over. You cannot simply add the habitat acreage objectives for each species and come up with a grand total acreage to manage for, because habitats for many of these species overlap considerably. If you manage an area for mallards, you'll automatically provide

---

[27] At the time of printing, there were 568 refuges.

some area for pintails as well, and vice versa. But how much? What about the third, fourth, and fifth species with somewhat overlapping niches?

The exercise of allocating conservation objectives from the national to the local level or, conversely, rolling them up from the local to the national, is crippled with complexity. Even if the FWS had the brains and the resources to handle such complexity, the task is never completed because areas change ecologically. Grasslands succeed into shrublands and forests, fire transforms them back again, marshes dry up, flooding resets river channels, invasive species bring unprecedented habitats, and of course the 800-Pound Gorilla is always on the prowl, tearing up landscapes here and dumping pollutants there.

And let's not even get started on climate change, except to mention that climate change is a 400-pound nephew of the 800-Pound Gorilla. In a fossil-fueled, greenhouse gas-emitting economy, GDP growth is the key variable in the rate of climate change. And nothing rules the identity of an ecosystem like climate. Rapid climate change means rapid ecosystem change. What's expected to be mallard breeding grounds this year can easily become a mallard stopover in a decade, and a wintering area in the foreseeable future, or just plain mallard-less.

Frankly, the notion of planning and managing for the conservation of all species—even limited to "trust species"—by coordinating among all the parties involved, on an ever-changing landscape, was pure folly. It would take omniscience and eons. The Fish and Wildlife Service is nowhere close to having either.

There are basically two approaches to overcoming the crippling complexity of landscape-level planning for biodiversity conservation. The first, which I championed as conservation biologist, was using the coarse filter of ecosystem conservation. We'd use the National Vegetation Classification System (NVCS) and set a standard goal for conserving ecosystems at an intermediate level of classification. In particular, I suggested focusing on the "formation" level of the NVCS and adopting the goal of 10 percent protection in the conservation estate (Refuge System, national parks, etc.). In other words, a minimum of 10 percent of each formation would be conserved, along with all the species and other elements of biodiversity that came with them.

It was a perfectly practical approach because formations were already mapped across the United States. Meanwhile, the 10 percent goal was widely considered appropriate given a combination of conservation biology principles (such as the species:area curve), political feasibility, fiscal realities, and ongoing coordination with other conservation agencies. And, over time, we could fine-tune our ecosystem conservation efforts down to the "alliance" level of the NVCS as national mapping efforts ensued pursuant to the National Vegetation Classification Standard, which had recently been adopted by the Federal Geographic Data Committee. Moving from the formation level to the alliance level would amount to applying a finer net over the coarse filter.

One by one, I won converts on the National Goals Team for the "coarse-filter approach." Ecosystem conservation was the state of the art in conservation biology, and I had a network of friends and colleagues in The Nature Conservancy (TNC), Natureserve (the vigorous science organization that spun off from TNC), the U.S. Geological Survey (USGS), and various Natural Heritage programs (state government operations) who strongly supported the idea and were willing to help us make it happen. We would have had relatively smooth sailing with this approach.

The other way to simplify things, which the Service attempted, is the "surrogate species approach." This approach is as it sounds: You choose representative species ("surrogates" as it were) for a host of other species—and focus on conserving them, presumably conserving the remainder of species in the ecosystem. It's basically the opposite of the ecosystem approach, and it failed miserably at FWS. Simply *talking* about the surrogate species approach—educating Service personnel about what it meant, persuading them it was the way to go, figuring out which species were to be designated as surrogates, and then determining how to use them for habitat conservation planning—cost taxpayers in more ways than one and for several years running.

The most obvious cost was the cumulative salary dedicated to all the talking and learning about the surrogate species approach. Virtually all of the biological positions in the Service had to take it up. And they didn't just take it up from where they sat. Many of them, perhaps even most of the workforce, wound up travelling for talks and training. Government travel is an expensive proposition for the taxpayer, to say the least (Chapter 10).

Some of the workforce—most notably layers of chiefs from Refuge System headquarters—travelled ad nauseum. The favored location was Alaska, especially in summer, just as Florida, California, and various points along the Gulf of Mexico were favored in winter. Apparently the chiefs needed to help each other adjust their thinking caps, and encourage one another that they were doing the right thing. With Dan Crasche kicking things off with his old football stories, the collection of chiefs convinced themselves that they were doing something "bold" and progressive, and incidentally something conducive to fine lodging and Bible Club beer parties out in God's greenest acres.

Then there were the opportunity costs. All that time spent spinning the wheels on surrogate species could have been used on the backlog of other pressing needs. Instead, projects long in the making were suddenly dropped. Fulfilling the Promise quickly became unfulfilling.

The inability of Crasche, Dirth, and their hand-picked sub-chiefs to handle the politics of ecosystem conservation helps to explain why, despite the incredible investment in Fulfilling the Promise, we found ourselves undertaking yet another visioning exercise within just a few years. Probably a bigger reason was that Crasche didn't feel he had enough ownership over Fulfilling the Promise. In fact, Fulfilling the Promise was viewed by Service employees as more of a Rick Coleman initiative.

Crasche wanted to reshape the agency to his own liking and, more importantly, to his own *credit*. Political appointees are driven to leave their mark, and ideally the mark will be akin to a patent or logo that adds to their fame and fortune for years to come. Fulfilling the Promise wasn't Crasche-centric enough, so a great deal of taxpayer resources went into an intensive and lengthy process of meetings, conferences, policy development, social media campaigning, and networking among partners, publics, and policymakers. The general effect was to erase the memories of Fulfilling the Promise and establish a legacy under the new logo, Conserving the Future.

The highlight of the social media campaigning and networking was the Bold Ideas Forum, which went online and public in February, 2011. It was supposed to be as it sounded: an open forum for ideas—bold ones—about what the Refuge System should actually *do* in the 21st century. The forum had a well-developed website where anyone could submit an idea, and visitors would vote for their favorites. Each visitor was allotted three votes and allowed to allocate them among three ideas. The voting system of the Bold Ideas Forum was supposed to be a unique and progressive form of democracy that would emanate a sense of fairness. It was supposed to make the participants feel truly involved and heard.

I could hardly exaggerate the exaggeration used by Refuge System leadership in calling staff to participate in the forum. On February 11, the Chief of the Refuge System emailed employees with the exhortation, "The bold ideas forum is a place to go wild intellectually, where you can add your push-the-envelope thinking on behalf of wildlife conservation." On March

2, a branch chief emailed the Division of Natural Resources and Conservation Planning, "[We] would not be doing our jobs if we didn't encourage all of you to be part of shaping the Vision document during the public review period... Please pay particular attention to the section called 'Bold Ideas.' Here's a place where your wildest dreams (well Refuge conservation dreams) can come true. Our division should take the time, energy and effort to propose truly innovative and bold ideas."

All of a sudden, thinking big and being bold were themes throughout the Refuge System. "Think big or go home" (Dan Crasche's favorite), "think outside the box," "don't hold back," "push the envelope," "go wild," "your wildest dreams..." It was as if the chiefs were trying to outdo each other with "daring" exhortation.

In retrospect, we had a staff that had been conditioned to toe the line, and Crasche probably felt there was little to fear from the minions. "Bold" wasn't saying much in that setting. Here and there were free thinkers, but most of them had given up on Service leadership. Some of these thinkers kept a foot in the door of academia, others were active in nonprofit organizations, and at least one fellow was deep into corporate networking, mining for conservation gold among the CEOs of Northface, Patagonia, and Esprit.

I, too, had largely given up on the Service as a serious conservation organization with the guts to deal with the political economy of conservation, at least at the headquarters level. I kept a foot in the door of academia as a visiting professor in the National Capital Region of Virginia Tech. I developed and taught courses in ecological economics, steady-state economics, endangered species policy and management, climate change, and wildlife management. I served on numerous graduate student committees, and most of my students got jobs in the conservation professions, including some as FWS employees. (Hopefully they remember their lessons in ecological economics.)

And, on nights and weekends, I ran CASSE. Then, starting in 2007, Rob Dietz ran CASSE, freeing me up for CASSE oversight, networking, and fundraising. By the time of the Bold Ideas Forum in 2011, CASSE was well-known in the environmental community, certainly in wildlife conservation circles. This was the same year CASSE won the "best environmental think tank" award.[28] CASSE was especially well-known among FWS leadership.

Several aspects of CASSE made it highly relevant to the FWS and the Bold

---

[28] This was an award issued by the organization Treehugger (treehugger.com), which is under different management than when the award was issued.

Ideas Forum. First, the CASSE mission hearkened back to Rick Coleman, the "original" Jamie Clark, and even to Lynn Greenwalt, the FWS director at the time the Endangered Species Act was passed. It invoked the historic, big-thinking traditions of Olaus Murie and Rachel Carson, FWS heroes.

Second was the Rob Dietz connection. He'd resigned from the FWS and taken a 40 percent pay cut to serve as CASSE executive director. He was highly respected and had a well-established network among FWS employees and partners.

Third, numerous FWS leaders from past and present—including Greenwalt—had signed the CASSE position on economic growth, which identified the "fundamental conflict between economic growth and environmental protection." At the time, the decision of whether to sign the CASSE position was something of a litmus test in ecological economics.

Fourth, friends of CASSE were active in the Bold Ideas Forum.

So, it was with an equal mix of trepidation and excitement that I submitted my "bold idea" to the forum. The title was "Raise public awareness of the trade-off between economic growth and wildlife conservation." Trepidation stemmed from the history of gag orders, reprimands, and suspensions. I was one of the few entrants who truly had to *be* bold—career-wise at least—to submit an idea.

Excitement stemmed from the fact that, for the first time in years, the door seemed open to dialog about the 800-Pound Gorilla. In fact, not only did the door seem open, the sky seemed the limit because the winning ideas would be guiding discussions of the new Refuge System vision at the culminating conference in Madison, Wisconsin. I was eager to return to my alma mater as part of the retinue from Refuge System headquarters, winning idea in hand.

The full text of my idea is provided on pages 68–69. While it was based on technical, ecological macroeconomics, the idea was essentially a public outreach proposal, as reflected by its title, "Raise public awareness…" It also entailed a significant element of inter-agency dialog. We, the U.S. Fish and Wildlife Service, were to bring our ecological macroeconomics to federal economists such as those in the Council of Economic Advisors.

Printed in its entirety below is the winning submission from the 2011 U.S. Fish and Wildlife Service "Bold Ideas Forum." The forum was promptly scrubbed from the internet on the day voting was scheduled to end (Earth Day) which fell during the latter stages of Dan Crasche's Senate confirmation hearings for the position of Director, U.S. Fish and Wildlife Service.

Raise public awareness of the trade-off between economic growth and wildlife conservation

The mission of the National Wildlife Refuge System entails public outreach and collaborating with others to ensure adequate maintenance of wildlife habitats and populations across the landscape. The success of this approach depends on identifying the issues for which outreach and collaboration is essential. At landscape, regional, and national levels, these issues include widespread, systemic challenges such as invasive species and climate change. For issues such as these, we perform public outreach and we collaborate extensively with government agencies, academia, and NGOs.

Yet there is a major issue we have avoided: economic growth.

Economic growth is increasing production and consumption of goods and services in the aggregate. It requires increasing human population and/or per capita consumption. The size of the economy is indicated by gross domestic product, or GDP.

GDP is a solid indicator of habitat and biodiversity loss. Due to the tremendous breadth of the human niche, the human economy grows at the competitive exclusion of nonhuman species in the aggregate. The wildlife profession has already engaged the issue of economic growth and has described a "fundamental conflict between economic growth and wildlife conservation" (TWS 2003:1). Technological progress does not reconcile this conflict, and in fact the conflict is exacerbated when technological progress is put in the service of economic growth (Czech 2008). Yet for various historical reasons citizens in developed countries are inclined to believe that economic growth may be reconciled with biodiversity conservation and other aspects of environmental protection (Dresner 2002, Daly and Farley 2010).

The trade-off between economic growth and wildlife conservation is an issue of sound science that is crucial to the mission of the Refuge System. However, the idea is not to preach to the public that "economic growth is bad," nor to lobby the policy maker to reform macroeconomic policy. Rather, the idea is simply to raise public awareness about the trade-off between economic growth and wildlife conservation. The public and policy makers can decide what to do based on that knowledge. (For example, if wildlife conservation is deemed important enough, then consumer preferences will be more aligned with conservation, and policy makers will lessen the pressure on fiscal and monetary levers.)

Numerous partners are available for collaborating on this issue, including the U.S. Society for Ecological Economics, Gund Institute, New Economy Network, Earth Economics, and Tellus Institute. These organizations work directly in the field of ecological macroeconomics. Many others are addressing the issue less directly and would likely engage more directly if a partner such as the Refuge System were involved. Most of the professional, scientific natural resource societies are engaged with the issue to some degree as well, and several have working groups or similar units devoted to working on the issue.

Several government agencies also have individuals and programs conducive to collaboration, especially the environmental and natural resources agencies but not limited to them. For example, the Government Accountability Office has expressed an interest in macroeconomic sustainability matters, as has the General Services Administration (2009). Eventually such diverse natural resources and other agencies should open dialog with economics agencies, such as the Bureau of Economic Analysis and the Council of Economic Advisors, for purposes of delivering accurate information on the relationship of economic growth to wildlife conservation and other important ecological objectives.

Despite the existence of other organizations that work in ecological macroeconomics, we cannot expect others to accomplish the goal without our participation and perhaps some of our leadership. The issue of unsustainable growth is large and systemic, and it will take a large number of individuals and organizations to provide the critical mass required for widespread public awareness. Also, none of the other organizations mentioned above (except The Wildlife Society) have addressed the issue of economic growth with a focus on wildlife conservation. Most of them deal more generally with sustainability and social justice.

This idea is not synonymous with estimating the value of natural capital and ecosystem services (Gowdy et al. 2010). Such estimating of ecosystem values is the primary concern for ecological microeconomics. Although both approaches are useful in wildlife conservation, microeconomics is largely about allocating resources more efficiently (such as knowing which habitats will receive the strongest, weakest, or no protection), while sustainability is a macroeconomic concern (i.e., habitat conservation in the aggregate).

Finally, this idea is not intended to supplant the idea submitted by Jimmy Fox, "Make the communication of environmental sustainability a high priority of the NWRS & USFWS." Rather, this idea complements Jimmy's idea by focusing on a central issue that must be communicated for purposes of environmental sustainability and especially wildlife conservation.

(Literature citations were provided at the Bold Ideas Forum. Here they are included at the end of the book.)

The Bold Ideas Forum was set up to run until Earth Day (April 22). There were 239 ideas submitted to the forum. It became a bit like a lengthy horse race on a crowded track. I suppose my horse could have been called 800-Pound Gorilla. He—or she, if you prefer—was clearly a well-built horse for the purposes of such a race. The idea was straightforward, put in reasonably plain language, and, unlike most ideas submitted to the forum, backed up with literature citations, giving it academic credentials.

800-Pound Gorilla won the race, eventually by a landslide, but for a long time there was serious competition and, almost surely, some tampering with the electoral process.

With any other set of issues, and with many other players, I would strongly resist the suspicion—much less raise it in a book—of tampering. We have too many conspiracy theories plaguing the nation already. But my experience with the 800-Pound Gorilla, the FWS, and the Bold Ideas Forum suggest it was highly unlikely that tampering *didn't* occur.

By "tampering," I am not accusing the FWS of literally changing the vote tally. The tampering would have been nuanced and opaque. For example, one of the website settings was adjusted in a way that made the proposal more difficult to find.

Visitors to the Bold Ideas Forum would find, front and center, a basic explanation of the forum and its purposes. Immediately below that, no scrolling necessary, the ideas themselves appeared, along with an invitation to "Vote here." Of course, as the collection of ideas grew, the vast majority were not immediately visible on the front page. Therefore, readers were offered several options for sorting through the ideas. For several weeks the default option was "Top" (for top-ranked ideas), which of course is highly intuitive for any type of polling, voting, or watching of a horse race.

You can guess the rest. After 800-Pound Gorilla collected enough votes to pass all the other horses, it was front and center at the forum, no scrolling necessary. You couldn't help but encounter it. Right there at a U.S. Government-sanctioned website for "bold ideas," you came face to face with the 800-Pound Gorilla! For a fleeting few days I was tempted to be proud again of the FWS, almost as when I first briefed the directorate.

Alas, any belief in the Service as a sincere adherent to the principles of American democracy was a fantasy fit for a fool. In a week or two the default sorting option was changed from "Top" to "Newest," such that the most recent idea submitted was front and center. This less intuitive default spoke loudly and clearly between the lines of the ideas. The suppressors didn't want 800-Pound Gorilla to have an audience and went out of their way to keep the gorilla in the corner and off the screen.

This led to the headlining of ideas that could hardly be called "bold." We had, for example, "Create a Photography Permit," "Online Applications [for job openings]," and "Fundraising Training." Some of the headliners were general sentiments such as "Capture Our History" and "Less Talk, More Toil." There were the commercially ambitious ("Create 'Refuge World' Theme Park"), the bizarrely worded ("As a leading echelon in earthly creatures we must lead wisely by protecting not killings of others"), and the hopelessly convoluted ("Classify land cover maps for all refuges on a 5-year cycle using consistent methods and classification…").

One after the next, ideas got plopped into the mix like so many spitballs on a chalkboard. Although many made sense at some level, few would qualify as "bold," and fewer yet as big-picture, visionary ideas. None captured the essence, vision, and core of conservation like "Raise public awareness of the trade-off between economic growth and wildlife conservation." 800-Pound Gorilla wasn't just a horse in the race; he (or she) was a workhorse, able to pull many of the other ideas along like a packtrain to Madison.

Unfortunately, the route to Madison was pockmarked with pitfalls. At various points in the race, when 800-Pound Gorilla was on a roll, the voting system malfunctioned, time after maddening time. I heard about it from so many people who tried to vote, I lost track. One has to wonder how many others tried to vote for 800-Pound Gorilla; surely I'd have heard only from a small fraction. Many participants who wanted to vote would finally have given up.

Knowing what I know today, in my opinion the most likely explanation for the "malfunctioning" of the Bold Ideas Forum is that it was engineered to buy some time. "Leadership" hoped for another, more competitive idea to be submitted, and probably helped with efforts to come up with such an idea. They failed.[29]

What else could explain such malfunctioning? The only other reasonable explanation would be poor performance of the software, and/or the staff involved in managing it. Yet that explanation seems far-fetched, because public relations was of utmost concern to the FWS. It was usually the top concern at headquarters, and I've never seen it emphasized more than during those months leading up to Crasche's Senate confirmation hearings.

So, despite ample capacity at FWS headquarters for flubbing things up,

---

[29] They certainly couldn't come up with a better, bolder idea, but they did find one with more of a built-in constituency that could be quickly mobilized for voting. The idea? Simply to create a migratory bird conservation stamp for wildlife observers (similar to the famous "duck stamp," but for nonhunters). Once that was posted at the Bold Ideas Forum, the voting system was suddenly "fixed" and the idea gained ground on 800-Pound Gorilla for a short time. Alas, it was a futile attempt and, in any event, would have been a milquetoast winner for a "bold" ideas forum.

the Bold Ideas Forum would not have been left to chance. In fact, the engineering of it was placed in the hands of a fellow who was, by all accounts, one of the more intelligent, tech-savvy people in the agency. He was, however, a card-carrying Bible Club convert. So, I'll probably never be able to prove it, and I wouldn't quite bet the house on it, but I do believe the voting system was tampered with to some significant degree, and it's entirely possible that only one or two people knew about it. It would have been justified with the rationale, "Czech was ordered not to be talking about economic growth, so we need to cut this off at the pass."

What a tangled web they wove at the old Bold Ideas Forum.

Ultimately, though, none of this book rests upon whether or not the U.S. Fish and Wildlife Service or any of its staff tampered with the Bold Ideas voting process, because the whole *concept* of the forum was ultimately corrupted. Ignominiously enough, the most obvious corruption took place on Earth Day. Earth Day was the deadline for voting, and by early the next morning, the forum had been scrubbed from the internet, Google cache and all. Only years later, with the development of dedicated archiving software, were "captures" of the forum findable online.[30]

Scrubbing the Bold Ideas Forum from the internet was clearly not the original intent. The broader Conserving the Future website was kept open for many months during the spring and summer of 2011, as political appointees, senior executives, and various aspirants inserted their pre-conceived notions about "trust species" and "strategic habitat conservation." You can bet the house that the Bold Ideas Forum would have remained front and center, if only the winning ideas had conformed to Bible Club doctrine and enhanced Crasche's chances with the Senate.

800-Pound Gorilla wasn't the only horse that Crasche and the Bible Club didn't like. In fact, of the 239 ideas submitted, three of the top four vote-getters—one might even argue all four—pertained to the 800-Pound Gorilla. My proposal, of course, was entirely, explicitly, and pointedly about the 800-pounder. Second place went to a proposal to prohibit mining on the Refuge System. Mining is a substantial sector of the economy, and a sector that many others depend upon for *their* growth. This proposal was at least tangentially related to the 800-pounder.[31]

---

[30] Results from the Bold Ideas Forum may be viewed via the internet archiving software, "Wayback Machine." See http://web.archive.org/web/20110412092438/http://ideas.americaswildlife.org/forums/96077-bold-ideas/topics/96693-my-bold-idea-for-wildlife-refuges-is-/filter/top .

[31] (As a "bold idea," it shouldn't have been all that compelling, because mining was rarely

The third-place idea was to prevent wolf control on Alaskan refuges. Of the top four ideas, this was the only one without a major connection to the 800-Pound Gorilla. That said, the proposal was an example of how ecological integrity (including natural populations of wolves) entails lower rates of some types of economic activity, such as caribou hunting (which is hardly insignificant to resident Alaskans).

Among the other 238 ideas submitted to the forum, one overlapped substantially with 800-Pound Gorilla, and it took fourth place in the voting. It was, "Make the communication of environmental sustainability a high priority." The author of this idea, Jimmy Fox, was one of the few big-picture thinkers in the FWS, and one of the few who was bold enough indeed to pitch a big idea at the forum.[32]

In retrospect, exposing one's ideas—to critique, to censoring, to censure—was probably the "boldest" part of the forum. Taken as a whole, the ideas themselves were milquetoast. Even my idea wasn't so "bold" in terms of the substance. It's not like I was proposing a communist revolution or storming of the Bastille. I wasn't even proposing an overthrow of Dan Crasche or an abolition of the Bible Club.

In fact, I wasn't even proposing any particular policy reform! I was only proposing to *raise public awareness* of the conflict between economic growth and wildlife conservation. By 2011, the conflict itself had been well-documented in the peer-reviewed, scientific literature, so the idea was consistent with "sound science," too.

So I'm not claiming to be Mr. Bold. Sure, I subjected my idea to critique at the Bold Ideas Forum, which probably took a smidgen of courage—or stubbornness at least—given my experience with the government. But frankly the forum turned out to be almost entirely supportive! There were 54 comments posted about 800-Pound Gorilla, and all but one or two were highly supportive. The comments demonstrated widespread and diverse support, from inside and outside the FWS. Representatives of professional, scientific societies such as The Wildlife Society, the American Fisheries Society, and the U.S. Society for Ecological Economics all provided support.

---

allowed on the Refuge System anyway. However, most of the participants in the forum weren't familiar with the applicable mining laws and policies.)

[32] As of 2023, Fox remains a beacon of hope in the U.S. Fish and Wildlife Service. His rare combination of knowledge, integrity, and big-picture thinking is reflected in his TedEX talk, "The Oldest Task in Human History." See https://www.youtube.com/watch?v=azGE-JKz-4jE&feature=em-share_video_user .

So did representatives from nonprofit organizations such as Friends of the Earth, Earth Economics, and the Coast Range Association.

The response of one Thomas Wayburn was succinct: "The Fish and Wildlife Service has a chance to reach a wide audience with this fundamental idea, namely, that economic growth is unsustainable and, beyond the point it has reached in the US and other developed countries, extremely harmful."

Another fellow, Jonathan Herz, posted one of the more insightful responses found anywhere at the Bold Ideas Forum: "The importance of reexamining our current economic decision-making process cannot be overstated. This approach needs to inform implementation of Executive Orders and the ways cost-benefit analysis and return-on-investment is considered in the Government. A collaborative effort across agencies will help move us in the right direction—towards sustainability. And, we need to start, now."

The diversity, intensity, and unanimity of support was something an agile politician could have capitalized on easily. But neither the bold idea nor the supportive comments comported with the preconceived and limited visions of Dan Crasche, Tim Dirth, and their Bible Club cultists. Evidently the politics were too hot to handle even for the likes of Crasche, who once boasted at a meeting, "I can drink politics from a firehose."

And so it was, that one of my greatest successes as a civil servant in raising awareness of the trade-off between economic growth and environmental protection became my greatest liability in the small-thinking FWS. The Bold Ideas Forum was scrubbed from the internet immediately after Earth Day, and just as immediately I started feeling the heat of retaliation. The first visit to my office was from the individual who would come to personify, for me, U.S. Government complicity in the win-win rhetoric that "there is no conflict between growing the economy and protecting the environment."

And now he had substantial control over my future.

8

REPRIMANDS, SUSPENSIONS, AND A RIGGED APPEALS PROCESS

Geoff Pudert was chief of the Division of Natural Resources and Conservation Planning for roughly the last nine years of my FWS career. He was mild-mannered, contemplative, and almost apologetic in his approach. These traits made him seem humble, and he was certainly well-liked, but I came to learn that Pudert's quiet demeanor had less to do with humility than a secretive cynicism.

Early on in Pudert's tenure, we had a lengthy and wide-ranging conversation. He knew of my efforts to raise awareness of the 800-Pound Gorilla, and he'd heard about some of the political difficulties I'd encountered. He described his own philosophy by quoting his late father: "Nobody gets out of this world alive." In the context of the conversation, he was essentially saying, "Why toil so hard for reform when you're not going to be around to see it come to fruition?" I recoiled a bit as I thought to myself, "What a way to remember your father."

Over the coming years, as a conservationist and taxpayer, I also became frustrated that we were paying the likes of Pudert the big bucks to get by with such a cynical attitude. He had advanced to division chief by automatically saying "yes" to everything from above, while saying "no" to everything from below that conflicted with anything from above. In other words, he was the quintessential yes man, and by 2016 he was the 55th–highest paid Fish and Wildlife Service employee with an annual salary of nearly $160,000 (nearly $200,000 in 2023 dollars).[33]

Pudert couldn't understand the passion I had for advancing the steady

---

[33] Pudert finally moved on to a higher level in the Department of the Interior, but the top 100 salaries of FWS employees are reported at https://www.federalpay.org/employees/us-fish-and-wildlife-service/top-100 .

state economy, with the sacrifices that entailed, when I could just go along for the Refuge System ride instead. Meanwhile he rode the Refuge System for all it was worth. Like many of the "chiefs," he traveled the country, indeed the world, all the while accumulating more and more in salary, bogus cash awards, and a particularly insidious form of corruption I'll describe as the "per-diem bonus" in Chapter 11.

Following the Bold Ideas Forum, Pudert was the first visitor to the last good office I held at the FWS. I mean "last good office" literally and figuratively. Literally, the office was in the physical middle of Refuge System headquarters. It wasn't luxurious or pretentious—it certainly wasn't one of the corner offices with a personal balcony—but it was a fairly spacious office with windows and, more importantly, it was situated perfectly for networking. I could see each and every person arriving and departing, visitors and staff alike, simply by turning my head to the right, where the 6th floor elevators were located. Yet I was far enough from the elevators to avoid being distracted by them.

Figuratively, my post as conservation biologist for the Refuge System carried the perfect position description as described in Chapter 2—perfect because it closely matched the skills I had worked hard to earn, and because it described a big-picture, long-term approach to conservation. It was just what the Service needed to address the conservation challenges of the 21st century. As the person who filled the position, I was still expected (outside of my chain of command, especially) to represent the Refuge System on big-picture issues. My expertise was still sought by progressive government programs, colleges and universities, and NGOs, on matters of biodiversity conservation and ecological economics.

All that was to change, and rapidly. My career was about to take a nosedive into a year-long nadir punctuated by a verbal reprimand, a written reprimand, a fresh gag order, and three suspensions. And those were only the formal damages.

Pudert began his visit by downplaying the significance of the Bold Ideas Forum and my winning idea. Despite the fact that, for the past four months we'd been exhorted to vote at the Forum, he stated slowly and incredibly, "It's not like it was a vote or something." Pudert wasn't particularly articulate, and in this case his statement was further crippled by the dishonesty thereof. The reality was, "it" (the victorious vote count) wasn't *like* a vote, because it was nothing *but* a vote. That's why "Vote here" was featured front and center at the forum!

With Pudert lurking in the doorway and hovering over the airspace, I suddenly felt a tinge of desperation. Here was a ladder-climbing, cynical bureaucrat discarding the truth in a way I had never seen before, at least not firsthand. Gradually the slow-paced conversation combined elements of interrogation with reprimand and coercion. I got the sickening feeling that my career was in serious trouble, that I was being set up for a long, bad ride.

The interrogation aspect pertained to the vote count. Pudert and the chain of command suspected I had tapped into the CASSE network to garner votes. It didn't take Sherlock Holmes to figure that one out. The bosses had exhorted us to get the word out. Who did they think we should get the word out *to*? The local bridge club? The National Football League? *Cigar Aficionado*? CASSE was an active and effective presence in the conservation world at the time, with a position on economic growth that had been signed by numerous leaders in the scientific, professional natural resources societies such as The Wildlife Society, American Fisheries Society, Society for Conservation Biology, and Ecological Society of America. E.O. Wilson, Jane Goodall, and David Suzuki were signatories of the CASSE position. Even a past FWS director had signed it![34] In fact, hundreds of FWS employees had signed the CASSE position.

Unlike the real FWS leaders who actually signed the position, Pudert sailed with the political winds. By the time of the interrogation, he'd probably already gotten his marching orders from Dirth to extinguish any talk of the CASSE position. For these purposes he also engaged an unscrupulous branch chief, Debra Pock, who'd become my immediate supervisor shortly before the commencement of the Bold Ideas Forum.

Pock was the alter-ego of Pudert, albeit with the same agenda. In contrast to the mild-mannered, mechanical Pudert, Pock had an explosive and unpredictable personality, and was prone to cast judgment on the spur of the moment. Yet, she was also capable of showing up the next day with a completely different attitude and approach. It was just my luck, having her as my only intermediary with the higher chain of command.

Pock was a classic example of the inbreeding characterizing Refuge

---

[34] Lynn Greenwalt, the seventh Director of the U.S. Fish and Wildlife Service, became a CASSE signatory on December 3, 2009. Greenwalt was Director immediately on the heels of the Endangered Species Act, and therefore familiar with the plight of species as a matter of rampant economic growth in the mid-late 20th century. He was also a progressive and dignified leader, the likes of which FWS has been missing ever since. (The 11th Director, Mollie Beatty, was evidently a similarly courageous leader, but her leadership was tragically cut short by cancer.)

System hiring practices. Without fail, new hires were buddies of Dirth or at least budding disciples of the Bible Club. Many of them were highly entertaining to Dirth, and vice versa. Pock had a loud, loquacious persona; she could drink beer and shout louder than any of the good ol' boys. She could be funny and a real pal, I'm sure, but if you were in her doghouse, she could be mean and abusive.

I hoped for the best and experienced the rest.

Years later one of my co-workers observed that Pock immediately cast judgment on several people when she got to headquarters. Several she would "just hate" thereafter, and several she would adore. My co-worker also noted that I was the most extreme example of the former, and it was "obvious" to everyone. Her response to the Bold Ideas Forum provided ample evidence of that, but her hatred was mixed with a sort of disoriented and disorienting confusion, too.

Pock's supervision of me included several earlier meetings that I interpreted as straightforward, heart-to-heart discussions about the 800-Pound Gorilla. She basically said, "Well, we have to follow orders," meaning the gag orders that had plagued me for nearly a decade by then. Yet for months she was clearly conflicted on the topic.

Pock's unpredictability was on full display at a weekly division meeting one Wednesday morning in 2010. She pointed to an article she'd just read about the growing human impact on the environment. Animated and tearful, she lamented the environmental state of affairs and passionately proclaimed, "This is what it's all about for us! This is what we need to be doing!"

I couldn't believe my ears, because the article was practically a manifesto for a steady state economy. Or at least the scientific build-up to such a manifesto. And I had at least ten witnesses, co-workers from the Division of Natural Resources and Conservation Planning. Yet I didn't push the issue; it was definitely not the time to say "I told you so." Instead I took her pronouncement to heart, and even felt sympathetic. She'd displayed what Aldo Leopold lamented a half century prior, that the ecologist "lives alone in a world of wounds." For some time afterward, I had the impression that Pock was, after all, a reluctant purveyor of the previous gag orders.

Then, in the midst of the Bold Ideas Forum, the "Carter Incident" transpired. Quickly the incident became well-known within FWS, as well as to my advisors at PEER (Public Employees for Environmental Responsibility). Unfortunately, it never became known to Jimmy Carter, who I am convinced would have come to the rescue.

The Carter Incident transpired on January 18, 2011. The setting was the National Conservation Training Center (NCTC) in Shepherdstown, West Virginia. The event was the 50th anniversary of the establishment of Arctic National Wildlife Refuge, the largest refuge and, at over 19 million acres, the largest terrestrial landholding in the United States. President Carter gave the honorary address, and the auditorium was packed. I was there and on a mission. I was determined to ask Carter the following, which I printed and brought to the event:

> Mr. President, my name is Brian Czech and I'm a conservation biologist for the Refuge System. We are all grateful for what you did with ANILCA [Alaska National Interest Lands Conservation Act], as well as your support for the Refuge System, the Endangered Species Act, and other conservation policies and programs. What gets less attention is that you read *Limits to Growth*, commissioned the follow-up, *Global 2000*, and even invited the great steady-state economist, E.F. Schumacher, to the White House. You recognized the trade-offs between economic growth and environmental protection.
>
> But for several decades now we've heard the rhetoric that "there is no conflict between growing the economy and protecting the environment." So I have two questions. Can you help us to raise public awareness of the trade-off between economic growth and environmental protection? Also, do you have any advice for how we can do our part to raise awareness of this trade-off?

I believe my question would have been well-received by Carter and the audience alike, with the exception of the Bible Club, of course. The question certainly warranted as much consideration as any of the other questions and comments that were raised. It had all the elements befitting such a setting: It was professional, respectful, and carefully prepared. It was non-redundant and brief, yet with just enough background to set the stage. And it was a bona fide question, not a statement masquerading as a question.

More importantly, Carter's response would have surely been wise, valuable, and worthy of careful consideration. He was not only a conservation hero and an early leader in sustainability affairs; he was intimately familiar with the issues, including the politics thereof.

Pock had encouraged me to attend the event but advised me to "keep it cool." The advice wasn't necessary; I wasn't naïve enough to make it hot. I did the homework and spent the time to craft a respectful question that was highly relevant in the context of the venue and the Bold Ideas Forum.

Yet with the benefit of hindsight I believe Pock, or someone in the chain of command, engineered a set-up to protect the Bible Club from any unnecessary exposure to the 800-Pound Gorilla.

The emcee was the director of NCTC, Jay Sack. When Carter was done giving his talk, Sack moderated questions from the audience while a couple of helpers traversed the auditorium with microphones. My hand was up fast enough to be one of the first in the queue. Sack looked straight at me a dozen times at least, but after every question and answer he would point to someone else. After the first question or two, I started using a white piece of paper to be doubly sure he saw me. After three or four questions, I even kept my hand (with the paper) up in the air. Finally, after about ten questions, one of the helpers made it over to where I was seated and handed me a microphone. As Carter finished responding to the preceding question (which, maddeningly, wasn't even a question but a drawn-out thank-you), I rose to ask my question about the 800-Pound Gorilla.

Suddenly, Sack swooped in to the podium and thanked President Carter for his time. The audience erupted in applause. Carter's security team surrounded him, escorting him up an aisle toward the back of the auditorium.

This was perhaps the most frustrating moment of my life. I was mere seconds away from a game-changing opportunity, mic in hand, and the rug was pulled out from under me. There is no doubt whatsoever that Carter's response would have dramatically altered the FWS approach to the 800-Pound Gorilla.

With the way the questions were moderated, and how the event ended, I knew something was fishy. Only later was I apprised by confidants that Sack was a central figure in "Bible Club North," or the NCTC manifestation of the Crasche-Dirth cabal. (NCTC had its own bar—craft beer, free popcorn and all—for Bible Club sessions.) But I had precious little time to speculate on what had just happened, because President Carter was almost to the back door of the auditorium.

Instinctively, I filed behind Carter's entourage and followed them out the door. I assumed Carter would be hosting discussions in the hallway and the adjoining lobby; I might at least get a chance to ask him the question in person, albeit unwitnessed by the audience. Instead, the group filed straight across the hallway and into a stairwell. Not knowing the layout of NCTC, I had no idea that the particular stairwell in question was used for escorting dignitaries out to their waiting limousines. Once in the stairwell, though, I began to understand that Carter was in exit mode, and that any chance to engage him was rapidly evaporating.

Carter was already down to the second flight of stairs—maybe two flights were left—and there were approximately ten individuals between him and me. Some of the group were talking among themselves and the President himself did not seem occupied with any of them. So I said in a slightly raised voice, "Mr. President?" hoping he would hear me above the other voices. I don't think he even heard me; he didn't look up and didn't miss a step. But that was the beginning of the Carter Incident, because the fellow immediately in front of me turned out to be "Officer Toomey."[35]

"Keith Toomey" was an FWS special agent who'd been loaned out to supplement Carter's Secret Service escort. He turned this civilian affair into a major case befitting a crime: investigation, file, and all. He was probably a wannabe Secret Service agent, and my friends at PEER got a good laugh out of his overly detailed "incident report," but it wasn't funny to me. The gross exaggerations in this official "report" allowed Roque and Pudert to deliver the knockout blow to my winning idea at the Bold Ideas Forum. And for all I knew, it marked me forevermore among the American security apparatus, precluding me from major political events and leadership. For some reason Pock repeated numerous times, "You're never going to get close to President Carter again."

Beyond that, "Toomey's" report turned out to be the perfect excuse for disciplinary action. Pudert and Pock were already dragging the Damoclean sword along the epidermis of my scalp; the additional weight of the Carter report drew blood from my career. After sitting on the report for months, waiting for an especially opportune time to keep me away from the office, Pock used it to suspend me for two weeks.

In addition to costing me nearly $3,000 (a heavy hit for a mid-level civil servant in the Washington, DC beltway), two weeks happens to be the longest suspension an employee may be subjected to without triggering access to the U.S. Merit Systems Protection Board. The MSPB is essentially the court of appeals for grievances filed by civil servants. My going before the board would have been too ironic—unacceptably so—for Pock, Pudert, Dirth,

---

[35] Special agents often operate via alias; therefore the quotation marks with "Officer Toomey." I knew one special agent in Arizona ironically named "Mike Luckino"—his luck ran out in the volatile business of ratites (ostriches, emus, and rheas), in which he partook on the side, losing tens of thousands of dollars in the process.

and Crasche. They were intent upon snuffing out any talk of the 800-Pound Gorilla, not allowing it into widening circles.

The Carter Incident triggered an avalanche of punitive and retaliatory treatment. Along with the suspension, I was issued the most draconian gag order I'd yet received. Pock prohibited me from saying anything or conducting "any activities related to economics." This new restriction was issued in the midst of Crasche's Senate confirmation hearings. Based upon a later conversation I had with Crasche, I believe the gag order originated with him, most likely verbally, and evolved into the written memo I ultimately received from branch chief Pock.

However it originated, I found this new gag order to be practically unworkable, given my involvement in projects pertaining to land acquisition priorities, climate change impacts, and ecosystem services valuation. All of these were "related to economics." Yet when I asked Pock for clarification, it was as if I had committed another offense in simply asking. The only clarification she provided was, "You know what I'm talking about."

It was clear that the deck was stacked so badly against me that there was no way to win. Sure, I knew that the crux of the gag order was to eliminate all talk of the 800-Pound Gorilla. But I also knew what the chain of command had amply demonstrated by then, that they would use any excuse to coerce me into resignation. Now that Pock had issued such a sweeping gag order, I could hardly do anything without running into trouble.

This was verified yet again when, a couple months later, I was suspended for supposedly being absent without advance notification. I documented how this was an error—I had in fact provided advance notification via email—but this wasn't enough for Pock. She turned to the rationale that my notification wasn't far enough in advance, anyway, and took the disproportionate approach of suspending me for two days. The suspension went on record with supporting documentation that was factually incorrect, but I knew it was fruitless for me to appeal.

A few months later, yet another "incident" occurred. By then my career was deep in shambles and I was frustrated, depressed, and humiliated. One might wonder why I didn't just quit, but I'm not a quitter. Not only that, by then I'd sunk much of my career into federal service, and I was only a few years short of eligibility for at least a small pension. Quitting then would have been an even heavier hit than I'd taken already. So I wasn't about to quit, but I was desperate for a different chain of command, and even for some reasonable company.

What saved me for the time being, somewhat ironically, was Pock's promotion to a position in the Hadley, Massachusetts regional office. Immediately afterward, another of Dirth's recruits, Sarena Selbo, took the Branch of Planning and Policy chief position at headquarters, and I was re-assigned to that branch.

For a short time at headquarters, Pock, Selbo, and a third Dirth recruit, Kim Trust, were all present at headquarters with adjacent offices. These were relatively young white women and Dirth got into the habit of calling them "Charlie's Angels," especially when inviting them to the Bible Club drinking hour(s).

During Selbo's first week in the office, Pudert had her suspend me for sending an email to Michael Bean, a DOI attorney. (I had a legal question about land ownership in cases of barrier islands that shifted with the sands). Bean, a wildlife law expert, had long known of my scholarship on the Endangered Species Act; he and I were two of a handful of authors who'd written books on the ESA. We'd discussed the 800-Pound Gorilla, too. There was no overreach on my part, but Pudert was looking for any excuse to add another disciplinary action to my file and push me closer to the door. Unlike Pock, who would have heartily obliged, I could see that Selbo was uncomfortable—even somewhat shocked, it seemed—when Pudert got the three of us together to issue the suspension through her.

For the next couple of years, Selbo and I co-existed in a somewhat tense but polite and respectful relationship. She never expressed much of an interest in ecological economics, but she was as smart and competent as anyone else in that chain of command. She was stable and considerate, too. Although she never gave me any slack with the 800-Pound Gorilla, she never went out of her way to "get" me and never falsely accused me of anything. She even got me out of "the closet" (the notoriously tiny, stuffy office I'd been relegated to by Pudert and Pock) and back into a decent office. I was so appreciative, I did my best to lay low during her tenure. My primary product during that period was *Planning for Climate Change on the National Wildlife Refuge System*, a hundred-pager including not only my own writing and editing but numerous chapters by scientists from FWS, other agencies, and academia.[36]

Now I did happen to include a paragraph or two in *Planning for Climate Change* about the tight relationship between GDP and greenhouse gas emissions. This could hardly be avoided in the introductory section on the causes

---

[36] The climate change primer is archived online by the USDA: https://www.fs.usda.gov/research/treesearch/49201.

of climate change. After all, the Intergovernmental Panel on Climate Change (IPCC) had described in some detail how GDP was a primary variable in climate forcing. Especially for federal documents, the IPCC was *the* source of background information on climate change.

Selbo was reasonable enough that my brief mention of GDP in *Planning for Climate Change* didn't put me in the doghouse, at least not under her watch. It did, however, under the "reign of terror" conducted by the next (and my last) branch chief. *Planning for Climate Change* became the newest baby thrown out with the bathwater. By then there were many, and there'd be a few more.

9

BABIES IN THE BATHWATER

OF THE 800-POUND GORILLA

The gag order is a spectacularly ham-handed approach to controlling communications. Not only do gag orders destroy morale and warp the sociology of the workplace; they inevitably have incidental effects on projects far beyond the scope of the gag orders. These include projects that even the smallest-minded appointees and chiefs would (or should) otherwise want addressed in their programs and chains of command. Such projects become the proverbial babies in the bathwater.

In this case, the bathwater metaphor is itself a frustrating irony. Why should raising awareness of the conflict between economic growth and wildlife conservation be considered "bathwater" to start with? Raising awareness of the conflict is clearly the right thing to do, pursuant to the mission of the FWS. The fact that such awareness-raising was tossed out for decades by Refuge System "leadership" does not make it bathwater. The only way the bathwater metaphor works here is to refer to raising awareness as "the (supposed) bathwater." Refuge System chiefs treated it (that is, raising awareness) as bathwater in need of tossing, and threw out plenty of babies therewith, but they were mistaken not only in the tossing of the babies, but perhaps more by tossing out the (supposed) bathwater.

In any event, this chapter is focused on the "babies."

The chapter began to materialize on August 30, 2017, while the devastating toll from Hurricane Harvey was coming into focus. The hurricane reminded me—as did Hurricane Irene in 2011 and Hurricane Sandy in 2012—of the biggest baby in the bathwater. That baby was climate change expertise, in particular related to sea-level rise and coastal flooding.

I'd studied the process and effects of climate change as part of my curriculum in the 1990s and brought my knowledge of these topics to Refuge

System headquarters. For roughly the first 10 years with FWS, in fact, I served as the de facto "climate change coordinator" for the Refuge System. One of my earliest efforts was to review the models available for sea-level rise planning, and select the one that would fit best with Refuge System needs and budgets. I settled upon the Sea Level Affecting Marshes Model, with the apt acronym "SLAMM."

In those earlier years there was still so much ignorance about climate change at headquarters that I found it nearly impossible to gain any traction for climate change planning. A key barrier was Erin Alberres, who we saw in Chapter 3 was also the biggest obstacle to incorporating land acquisition costs in land acquisition planning. He was a climate change denier who eventually was forced to give in as climate change became a common theme among the natural resource agencies by the end of President Bush's second term. Unfortunately, by then many a land acquisition dollar had been unwisely spent on low-lying coastal properties, especially in Florida. Many of these properties were absolutely vulnerable—and predictably so—to sea-level rise. Yet Alberres refused to budge, and the rest of the Bible Club did nothing to hold him accountable.

Yet another early obstacle to progress on climate change and sea-level rise was Dick Schultz, the Bible Club branch chief cited in Chapter 2 who conflated centimeters with millimeters. Schultz loved to stifle progress if he couldn't reconcile it with his hook-and-bullet vision. Because the hook-and-bullet vision was the only one he practiced, he saw it as the only "practical" approach to the world. The bigger picture was beyond the pale; a few millimeters at a time was all he could handle.

Not all of the early opposition to climate change and sea-level rise planning came from headquarters, though. Some coastal refuge managers, especially in the South, did their best to undermine the accounting for sea-level rise in land acquisition planning. The opposition from these southern managers had little to do with any cultural or political divide between them and Refuge System headquarters. Rather, the opposition emanated from the South simply because the southern Atlantic Coast and especially the Gulf of Mexico have the most extensive coastal marshes and shorelines.

Of the 172 coastal refuges, dozens dot the coastlines from Texas to the tip of Florida and up the Atlantic seaboard to the Carolinas. Furthermore, this region has the most pronounced sea-level rise problem due primarily to its geological and hydrological features. The implications of SLAMM analysis were particularly severe for land acquisition at these refuges.

It wasn't hard to understand and even empathize with managers who'd spent years and even decades developing close ties with coastal communities. In some cases these managers had carefully cultivated the trust of locals and had finally reached tentative agreements for acquiring prime wildlife habitats, most notably coastal marshes with rich populations of migratory birds. It must have been difficult to give up on acquiring lands they'd coveted for years, and many of them never did give up. Nevertheless, they shouldn't have ignored so readily the "sound science" that supposedly drove Refuge System decisions.

Yet another barrier to sea-level rise planning was a handful of USGS scientists who seemed envious that anyone in FWS would have the audacity to plan for sea-level rise without consulting them frequently, using their models, and even funding their research. This isn't the book for details on sea-level rise modeling or comparing the available models but suffice it to say that only SLAMM met the criteria for a workhorse model for Refuge System sea-level rise planning. The USGS modeling pushed by the likes of Glen Guntensbergen, Don Cahoon, and colleagues was notoriously time-consuming, expensive, and virtually useless for practical land acquisition and management decisions. This became abundantly evident to all who familiarized themselves with the options, but the USGS scientists were a prime example of letting perfection—and big-funding pipe dreams—get in the way of progress. Meanwhile their self-serving complaints about the imperfections of SLAMM caused unnecessary and lengthy delays of widespread SLAMM analysis.

Despite all the barriers, and with occasional help from unexpected quarters (most notably a consortium called the Gulf of Mexico Alliance, plus a handful of particularly progressive refuge managers), I persevered with SLAMM analysis. The outcome was that by 2013 we had procured for the Refuge System a SLAMM analysis of every refuge for which it was relevant and meaningful.[37] That amounted to 132 of the 172 coastal refuges.

SLAMM analysis was clearly going somewhere, and fairly fast for government work. Acceptance of SLAMM among refuge managers had gradually become widespread, along with the grudging respect of most of the relevant scientists in academia and the USGS. We had also assisted with substantial upgrading of SLAMM itself. And we'd collaborated with the National Wetlands Inventory in the development of the online "SLAMM-View," an

---

[37] Czech, B. 2015. Coastal planning on the National Wildlife Refuge System with the Sea Level Affecting Marshes Model (SLAMM). *Wetland Science and Practice* 32(2):30-40.

interactive platform for helping citizens, communities, and policymakers envision areas of concern under various potential sea-level rise scenarios.

There was plenty more to go, however. For example, we needed to update some of our earlier SLAMM analyses, which were based on a less refined model, and then enter into a phase of periodic updates—"re-SLAMMing" we called it. Updating is necessary as better data becomes available, as models improve, and as major storms impact coastal areas, re-writing the wetland maps in matters of minutes.

We also needed to compile our individual SLAMM analyses and publish collective reports for purposes of flyway and Refuge System-wide planning. In fact, we had a manuscript almost to the finish line that provided SLAMM results from the entire set of Atlantic Coast refuges. This manuscript was pregnant for publication when the "reign of terror" arrived.

Arun Lyze took over for Sarena Selbo in late 2015. In our very first meeting, informal as it was, Lyze was all smiles and highly congratulatory over the recently completed *Planning for Climate Change*. Yet overnight, it seemed, the Bible Club got to him and he took his marching orders to an unprecedented level of hostile suppression. Only a few short weeks after Lyze's congratulations, he called me into his office to inform me that, going forward, *no* work would be allowed on climate change! This was a stunning development. If my government career was to leave any sort of mark aside from the 800-Pound Gorilla or the Carter Incident, it should have been my body of work in climate change analysis, planning, and leadership. Instead, Lyze quickly converted my position into that of a boring-topics specialist mixed in with mind-numbing secretarial work.

Among the dozen supervisors I experienced firsthand at FWS headquarters, they saved the worst for the last. Lyze spent long hours joking and laughing with visitors to his office, and enjoying the good life of Refuge System travel as far as he could take it. But, in my opinion—an opinion borne of extensive experience in dealing with Lyze—he was smallminded and meanspirited. Unlike Selbo, who reluctantly held me to the fire with regard to the 800-Pound Gorilla, Lyze seemed to relish the power he was given to squeeze any significance out of my career.

Lyze was also one of the least gifted supervisors I'd had, which made his abusive treatment all the more frustrating. He constantly made mistakes in written communications, especially, yet would try to "correct" my writing whenever he (usually mistakenly) thought he had a chance.

In my opinion people can be measured by how they treat the less fortunate among them. It isn't admirable or edifying if someone is nice, friendly, and helpful only to those in a position to help with promotions, raises, and travel arrangements. But that's exactly how Lyze rolled, both in my experience and as corroborated by several of his past and concurrent co-workers.

Lyze or no Lyze, the dropping of my climate change work was stunning in its stupidity and a betrayal of public trust. Forty percent of the American population lives along a coastline—in counties directly on the shoreline—much of which is highly vulnerable to sea-level rise and coastal flooding from severe storms. With the SLAMM analysis program, we had something important to say, not only about the durability of wildlife habitats along the coast, but about the very safety and economic security of the coastal public. The SLAMM work should have been highlighted and circulated to local and regional authorities and the media. It should have been used to inform and warn counties such as Aransas, towns such as Rockport, and cities such as Houston (all in Texas) of the perils of pushing for ever more development in areas so clearly—as shown with SLAMM—vulnerable to the effects of sea-level rise and associated catastrophic storms.

It's not that FWS was the only game in town for educating these communities on climate change and sea-level rise. Yet articles such as "Houston's 'Wild West' Growth" (*Washington Post,* August 29, 2017) and books such as *Bayou Farewell* were testimony to the lack of knowledge and planning for sea-level rise among our southern coastal towns and cities. These populations needed all the information they could get from colleges and universities, USGS, the National Oceanic and Atmospheric Administration, the Gulf of Mexico Alliance, state agencies, FWS, and anyone else who could help with sound science and insights. This will be the case for decades to come, too.

The fact is, though, that none of the other agencies have the presence and connection with local communities along the coast that FWS does, due to its refuges dotting the coastlines and its possession of high-quality data. FWS and in particular the Refuge System should be playing a leading role in sounding the alarm for coastal publics vulnerable to intensifying coastal storms, flooding events, and ultimately sea-level rise. My work with SLAMM was perfectly suited for these types of warnings.

Instead, Refuge System "leadership" treated SLAMM analysis as a cousin to the 800-Pound Gorilla. It was too close a cousin for the comfort levels of the Crasches, Dirths, Puderts and the rest who were more concerned with their titles, perks, and Bible Club membership than leveling with taxpayers who needed the knowledge we possessed. As Gus Speth would lament about the U.S. government at large, "They knew."[38]

By the 2010s they knew very well—these Refuge System chiefs—about the perils of climate change and sea-level rise. And by then they knew all about the 800-Pound Gorilla, too. Yet they chose to suppress the most salient facts rather than bring them to the fore.

Another body of work thrown under the bus was the sustainability "roundtables" that were prevalent in the early 2000's. These roundtables consisted of representatives from various federal agencies, universities, and well-connected consulting firms. They were meaningful examples of the interdisciplinary thinking that was all the rage for about two decades among the natural resources professions, culminating with the Roundtable on Sustainable Forests.

The Roundtable on Sustainable Forests was established pursuant to the "Montreal Process," an outgrowth of the 1992 Earth Summit. The Montreal Process was all about monitoring 7 criteria and 54 indicators to help its 12 member countries stay alert to the condition of their temperate and boreal forests. The roundtable was convened and administered by the U.S. Forest Service, and I was recruited to help provide monitoring schemes for the biodiversity indicators and to help interpret known trends in forest biodiversity.

I served on the roundtable for several years before the gag orders crept in, and I helped author the *National Report on Sustainable Forests* (USDA 2004). The Montreal Process indicators included economic variables such as income from timber, which was often described as contributing to economic growth. Therefore, I insisted that the report include an adequate description of the conflict between economic growth and biodiversity conservation. To the best of my knowledge the *National Report* is the only published government document to acknowledge the conflict between growth and conservation. You'll find this acknowledgment—just a few sentences—on page 86 of the report, which was rolled out with great pomp and circumstance by the U.S. Forest Service.

Not that it was easy to get those few sentences included. President George W. Bush had just appointed Mark Rey, a timber industry lobbyist, as Undersecretary for Natural Resources and Environment in the Department of Agriculture. This put Rey in charge of the Forest Service; a classic example of the fox guarding the henhouse.

---

[38] Speth, J.G. 2022. *They Knew. The US Federal Government's Fifty-Year Role in Causing the Climate Crisis*. MIT Press. 304pp.

Rey was a bit player in American politics who never rose higher than his undersecretary role. Yet some of the Forest Service "leaders" on the roundtable were intimidated by his appointment. I'll never forget the wide-eyed Rich Guldin (the team leader) when he warned of Rey, "He's not bluffing." Evidently Rey had insisted on a pro-growth report, or Guldin assumed he wanted a pro-growth report, and just to be safe, he didn't want anything about the conflict between economic growth and biodiversity conservation in the report. Fortunately my co-author of the chapter on interpreting the indicators was David Radloff, a fellow of great integrity. He was just high enough in the ranks of the Forest Service to prevail in the argument over whether or not to acknowledge the conflict between growth and conservation.

Why was the outcome so different with the Roundtable on Sustainable Forests? Why, unlike in the FWS, were we able to muster the fortitude to acknowledge the conflict? In addition to the difference in the individuals involved, an interagency roundtable provides more political cover than availed by a single agency. With a roundtable, the accountability for controversy can be shared among a number of players rather than directed to a single director. Also, a roundtable leader isn't entirely empowered—psychologically or sociologically—to trump the inputs of representatives from other agencies.

There was no good excuse for shrouding the truth at FWS headquarters, but if Refuge System chiefs couldn't handle the truth about the 800-Pound Gorilla, they should have sent me out further on the roundtable circuit. I could have performed the other duties of conservation biologist while also frequenting the roundtables and gradually raising government awareness, at least, about the conflict between economic growth and environmental protection. This was a distinct possibility, and two years after joining the Roundtable on Sustainable Forests, I also joined the Roundtable on Sustainable Rangelands. There was by then a robust literature on rangeland health indicators that could be monitored and interpreted for sustainability purposes, and I was up on the literature. One of my Ph.D. committee members, George Ruyle, helped write the book on *Rangeland Health*, which I'd studied in detail, and I'd assisted in the development of range management plans for the San Carlos Apache Tribe. So I fit in fine with this roundtable, and furthermore the work was highly relevant to fulfilling the ecological integrity policy of the Refuge System.

Next I was in line (along with one other Refuge System staffer) for the Sustainable Water Roundtable, which had broad applicability to Refuge System affairs. Yet about this time Refuge System leadership woke up to the fact that I could also use these roundtable settings to raise awareness of the 800-Pound Gorilla, and by then Tim Dirth had made it his pet project to extinguish any such prospects. Therefore, I was prevented at the last minute from joining the water roundtable, and even pulled summarily from the forest and rangeland roundtables.

Given the metaphor of the chapter, we might say that a promising set of triplets—all three roundtables—were thrown out with the (supposed) bathwater.

Finally we come to perhaps the nicest baby of all, stillborn in the same crowded (and mis-named) bathwater. In 2009 a rumor circulated that the renowned Harvard scientist, E.O. Wilson, had an active interest in getting a national park established in the Mobile-Tensaw Delta, along the Gulf Coast in Alabama. Wilson was getting up there in age—80 at the time—and the establishment of a Mobile-Tensaw Delta National Park was at the top of his bucket list. (He would pass away in 2021.)

Wilson knew the delta like the back of his hand, for the delta was his childhood stomping grounds. As a 20th century child of the South, he was the Tom Sawyer of the plant and animal kingdoms, and he took his wonderment to astounding academic heights. His legendary knowledge of insect taxa, especially, was borne and nurtured in the fields, forests, and floodplains in and around the delta. Nearing a century later, having explored the depths of biodiversity over much of the world, he recognized the delta for the prize it was; that is, one of the last great biodiversity hotspots in the United States.

Next to E.O. Wilson, I was in entomological kindergarten, yet I had a well-developed knowledge of American biogeography, and I too knew the delta to be not only a biodiversity hotspot, but one of the last big American river deltas with substantial ecological integrity. Not only that, my special interest in economic geography pointed to the delta as an area with low land prices. Uncannily, owing to the relatively unfettered flow of sediments, the delta was also one of the least vulnerable areas to sea-level rise along the entire Gulf Coast. The prospects for conservation land acquisition here were almost too good to be true: big-time conservation benefits coupled with modest prices and rare resistance to sea-level rise!

I also knew Wilson was set up for disappointment, because there was no way in hell the locals of southern Alabama were going to allow a national park to be established in their midst. They too loved the delta: for hunting, fishing, and power-boating! With rare exceptions, national parks don't allow hunting or power-boating, and fishing is often prohibited or substantially curtailed.

I knew what had to be done. We (meaning myself and whomever I could get to help) needed to get E.O. Wilson on board with establishing a Mobile-Tensaw Delta National Wildlife Refuge instead. Unlike a national park, a refuge was something the locals could appreciate and support. Hunting and fishing are actually encouraged on a typical national wildlife refuge, and the existence of a refuge means that hunting and fishing should last "forever." Power-boating would probably be kept out of the backwaters, but would still be allowed in the main channels where it was most in demand. The locals would have appreciated this balanced approach to boating in the delta.

The beauty of the project was that so much of the needed public support had already been garnered by groups who'd been keen on the national park idea. Local and national conservation organizations, scholarly academies, county and state park authorities, and numerous local dignitaries (most notably Wilson himself) were all for protecting the delta. Unfortunately, anyone who studied the situation thoroughly enough came to the same conclusion: A national park was dead in the water. A Mobile-Tensaw Delta National Wildlife Refuge, then, was the million-dollar answer to the vexing question of how to protect this biodiversity hotspot.

In 2009 I still had a reasonable amount of autonomy at Refuge System headquarters. I still ran the Conservation Biology Program, and I was keeping my ecological macroeconomics largely confined to Virginia Tech and CASSE business on nights and weekends. While constantly monitored at FWS for any activity pertaining to the 800-Pound Gorilla, I was otherwise and generally free to operate in the realm of land acquisition planning, climate change assessment, sea-level rise planning, ecological integrity assessments and the like.

So, I worked my way into E.O. Wilson's network, and broke through quickly once he and his key associate of the time, Neil Patterson, realized the position I was in and the assistance I could provide. I was surprised by the relative lack of knowledge on their part about the FWS and the National Wildlife Refuge System, but these fellows were nothing if not fast learners. They met me one fall day of 2009 at a tavern in Washington, DC, and I gave them the basic pitch. They then invited me to Wilson's lab at Harvard, where we met at length over a two-day period. By the time I left Boston, "Ed" and Neil were fully on board with the idea of striving no longer for a national park, but rather for a Mobile-Tensaw Delta National Wildlife Refuge.

Not long after the Harvard meetings, Ed and I and a loose-knit team of ecologists met in Mobile for several events and field trips designed to familiarize the team and certain key guests with the wonders of the Mobile-Tensaw Delta. Then we met again for more of the same, and started getting into some fairly advanced planning with aerial, ground, and water explorations of the delta ecosystem, areas of exceptional conservation concern, areas to be considered for additional designation (such as my pitch for an E.O. Wilson Wilderness Area), and potential refuge boundaries. Almost everything was pointed in the right direction. I was happy for Ed, proud of the conservation network around the delta, and—for one of the last times in my federal career—excited about the work I was doing for biodiversity conservation. The refuge would be no postage stamp for puddle ducks, but rather the single most biologically diverse landholding in the United States! Playing a leading role in the establishment of such a refuge was on *my* bucket list, too.

Yet another heart-wrenching disappointment was in the works. This time, it didn't come straight from the headquarters chain of command. Rather, FWS staff from Region 4 (the Southeast) committed a serious faux pas and cost us all—FWS, the conservation community, and Americans at large—the Mobile-Tensaw Delta National Wildlife Refuge.

Regional realtors, managers, and planners, along with some counterparts from the State of Alabama, badly wanted to expand the Cahaba River National Wildlife Refuge in north-central Alabama, but they failed to follow protocol pertaining to public outreach. When their efforts to expand the refuge were discovered, a wealthy and well-connected adjacent landowner became enraged and cried foul all the way to the governor's mansion. Senator Shelby (Republican from Alabama) was outraged as well. It was a colossal failure to communicate with the public and key policymakers. The governor (as I recall it was the recently elected Robert Bentley) made it clear that no new refuge lands—*none*—were to be approved on his watch by the State of Alabama. The sudden prohibition applied to the expansion of existing refuges as well as the establishment of new ones.

In matters of field-based wildlife conservation, I've never seen such a dramatic shift in outlook. Literally in a matter of minutes, the Mobile-Tensaw Delta National Wildlife Refuge was yanked off the table. I was sad for Ed, and the thrill I'd had over the project shriveled into irrelevance as fast as a pin-pricked balloon.

But there's more to the story, more that's relevant to the 800-Pound Gorilla and the gag orders that shrouded it. The year 2009 wasn't the first time I'd talked with Ed Wilson. We'd met no later than 2001, when I tracked him down after his John H. Chafee Memorial Lecture at the National Council for Science and the Environment conference in Washington, DC. That was the first time I put a bug in his ear about the conflict between economic growth and biodiversity conservation. Back then, he was running with the win-win rhetoric of the Clintonian crowd, but it was clear he hadn't studied his ecological macroeconomics. That just wasn't in his wheelhouse at the time.

The next time I met him, circa 2005, we revisited the relationship between economic growth and biodiversity conservation. By then the CASSE position on economic growth had been widely circulating in venues he frequented. Now he was agnostic about the 800-Pound Gorilla, but that was progress. He was no longer touting the win-win rhetoric.

E.O. Wilson's stance on economic growth was important because the Society for Conservation Biology, Ecological Society of America, American Fisheries Society, and other scientific associations were considering adopting positions on economic growth. The CASSE position served as the starting point in the considerations of each of these organizations. Although the CASSE position had already been endorsed by prominent scientists from each of these organizations, including several past presidents, none of these individuals had the cachet of Ed Wilson. Ed was far and away the top conservation biologist in the United States, if not the world, and on this there was virtual consensus. If Ed said, via CASSE, that there was a conflict between economic growth and biodiversity conservation, it would be a game-changer for what I was calling the "new conservation movement"—that is, conservation pursued via macroeconomic policy reform.[39]

Ed's signature would also up the ante on Refuge System gag-ordering. Although Tim Dirth had unthinkingly blurted, "Everybody knows there's a conflict between economic growth and wildlife conservation," he was way off. In fact, even at Refuge System headquarters I found objectors to be nearly as common as supporters. Ironically, by 2005 or so, Dirth himself had "caused" much of the ignorance at FWS headquarters, in the sense that he (and Dan Crasche) had undermined or eliminated opportunities to learn. If Ed had signed the CASSE position at the optimal time (approximately 2005) it might have tipped the scales such that the conflict between economic growth and wildlife conservation would have been addressed in FWS training modules and leadership talks.

---

[39] Czech, B. 2007. The foundation of a new conservation movement: professional society positions on economic growth. *Bioscience* 57(1):6-7.

That didn't happen, but by the time we met at his Harvard laboratory, the 800-Pound Gorilla had been percolating in Ed's mind for nearly a decade. You can probably guess the rest of the story, or at least the bottom line, because that's where Ed finally signed.

Did Ed sign the CASSE position on economic growth as a political maneuver to appease me, such that I might work harder toward getting the Mobile-Tensaw Delta National Wildlife Refuge established? Who doesn't expect the occasional quid pro quo? Yet Ed Wilson was no mere politician. He was a first-class scientist of impeccable standards and integrity. He would never have signed the position without his thorough concurrence.

The only element of quid pro quo may have been Ed's willingness to read the position to begin with. In the past he'd avoided it, somewhat like the plague. Therefore, it came as a shock when *he* actually brought the topic up as we met in his lab. He was prepared to revisit the issue, and he knew I was as well. I had the position with me, of course (as I always did), and he read its 16 sentences carefully, stopping to comment or inquire about particular clauses. He found himself disagreeing with nothing, and agreeing wholeheartedly instead. So he signed the position and CASSE (through Rob Dietz, CASSE's executive director at the time) tactfully announced the news via press release. I didn't rub it in the noses of anyone at FWS, but the FWS certainly heard about it. Refuge System chiefs, in particular, didn't quite know what to do about it: It fell firmly in the gray area for even their hyperactive application of the gag orders.

Unfortunately it came to pass that, while Conserving the Future and the Bold Ideas Forum were leaving their scars on my career, Region 4 was blowing it in Alabama. Although my own body of work on the Mobile-Tensaw Delta project would have been deemed wildly successful had it been performed by any of the Refuge System chiefs, headquarters leadership was after my scalp as usual. The chiefs knew I'd managed to get Ed's signature on the CASSE position, and they knew the project had gone down in flames. Rather than calling out Region 4, they assumed and insinuated I was somehow to blame, and I was ingloriously prohibited from further work on the project and even further contact with Ed. Yet no one else from FWS took the time to explain to him what had happened; how Region 4 had blown it. The sudden silence must have befuddled Ed, and probably left him with a bad taste in his mouth.

In retrospect, there was surely another reason for the Refuge System chiefs to abruptly cut the line of communication between myself and Ed. By then, full planning was underway for the Conserving the Future conference in Madison. For a brief time, I'd received grudging support for talking with Ed about the prospects of him delivering the keynote address. No one else in the Refuge System was corresponding with him, and as the conservation biologist for the Refuge System, it was natural for me to be the one having these talks with him.

Yet it must have been around the same time when the chiefs caught on to the fact that Ed had signed the CASSE position. Just as they'd feared that Jimmy Carter would have issued a game-changer statement, and therefore kept me from accessing Carter at all costs, they feared E.O. Wilson would do the same in Madison. Therefore, they severed my ties with him, and they didn't establish their own.

If the Mobile-Tensaw Delta National Wildlife Refuge wasn't a baby thrown out with the (supposed) bathwater, a rousing speech by the world's leading conservation biologist was. Instead and by most accounts, the Madison speakers lineup turned out to be underwhelming, forgettable, and marked with the bureaucratic inbreeding that produced the likes of the Bible Club, the LAPS team, and the per-diem bonus.

Plenty of other examples could be cited whereby the baby was thrown out with the (supposed) bathwater, but the picture is clear by now. Refuge System leadership, from Dan Crasche to Tim Dirth and down to the division and branch chiefs, were collectively so intent on suppressing me and hiding the 800-Pound Gorilla that they undermined *any* projects and events—no matter how meritorious—with *any* connection to Gorilla. They made it a disgraceful habit; throwing the taxpayers' babies out with the (supposed) bathwater. They got it stuck in their minds that, "We must prevent Czech, with disciplinary force, from doing anything having to do with economic growth," and didn't have the integrity to back off even as it became ever-more apparent that wildlife conservation is *all about* dealing with economic growth.

Part Three

REFORMING THE U.S. FISH AND WILDLIFE SERVICE

Government exists for the interests of the governed, not for the governors.

Thomas Jefferson, *Thomas Jefferson Foundation Archives*

Whenever the people are well-informed, they can be trusted with their own government.

Thomas Jefferson, *Letter to Richard Price Paris*

10

JOY-RIDING ON TAXPAYER DOLLARS:

A REFUGE SYSTEM TRAVELOGUE

By now we have seen how the leadership of the National Wildlife Refuge System hid the conflict between economic growth and wildlife conservation. We've seen how political appointees and higher-level bureaucrats abused their authority. And we've seen how my career was perennially crippled by gag orders that formed a shroud, more opaque every year, over the 800-Pound Gorilla. Perhaps no other career in the annals of the U.S. Fish and Wildlife Service has been so thoroughly stymied, or any other topic so thoroughly suppressed.

We've also seen how suppressing the 800-Pound Gorilla affected other work of the FWS. Climate change, land acquisition, reform of the National Environmental Policy Act, biodiversity accounting, and other key topics and programs were hamstrung by the same Refuge System clique.

It must be emphasized that not all FWS programs are predisposed to ignore or evade the topic. To the contrary, I'm convinced a majority of civil servants at FWS and in the broader Department of the Interior are eager for awareness of the trade-off between economic growth and environmental protection. They want and need greater awareness among themselves, the public they serve, and the policymakers they report to and advise. Many of these people would be pressed to define the phrase "economic growth"— they've been prevented from even hearing about it in the context of their own work—yet they have a sense that it is indeed the 800-Pound Gorilla that blocks them from achieving real conservation. They want to see it clearly, understand it, and do something about it.

When I sent my open farewell letter to FWS employees on February 7, 2018,[40] warning the public about FWS corruption and exhorting the

---

[40] The letter to FWS employees was subsequently posted as "Farewell to FWS – Goodbye

FWS workforce to take on the 800-Pound Gorilla, I received dozens of responses. They were almost unanimously supportive, with many individuals expressing a desire to get more involved. One FWS employee immediately wrote a follow-up piece for the CASSE blog.[41] Another changed his official government signature line to include, "In a world of finite resources, the ideology of perpetual economic growth is an intellectually bankrupt paradigm that endangers all life on earth." The FWS historian asked to conduct an oral history of my career, and noted how Olaus Murie (one of the great wildlife conservationists) had been suppressed in his FWS career as well. (A better-known example, of course, was Rachel Carson, who had to quit FWS to write *her* book, *Silent Spring*.)

So it bears repeating that it was but a clique of Refuge System chiefs at headquarters—the Bible Club—that quashed every reasonable effort to raise public awareness of the conflict between economic growth and wildlife conservation. The Dirths, Puderts, Pocks, and Lyzes were suppressors par excellence.

It also bears repeating that, while there was abundant ignorance of ecological economics in FWS, there was no meaningful disagreement about the conflict between economic growth and wildlife conservation at the higher levels of the agency. As Dirth blurted, "Everybody knows there's a conflict between economic growth and wildlife conservation." So, the suppression had nothing to do with technical merits.

The gag orders weren't politically affiliated, either. Neither Dirth nor Dan Crasche, who thought he could "drink politics with a firehose," were pandering to a particular party. The win-win rhetoric of "no conflict" was common to Democratic and Republican administrations alike. It was patently false in a bipartisan way, "everybody knew" it was false, and sound science had refuted it for good measure.

If the gag orders stemmed from neither technical disagreement nor party politics, *then why were they issued*? The answer is an indictment of an agency gone astray or, more accurately, led astray by the Bible Club. It went far enough astray to warrant the label of corruption.

Corruption isn't always as cut and dried as, for example, nepotism or embezzlement. For 18 years I watched chiefs come and go at headquarters,

---

to Gag Orders" at https://steadystate.org/fws-gag-orders/.

[41] See "Conflict of Interest at the U.S. Fish and Wildlife Service? A Deal Some Couldn't Refuse" at https://steadystate.org/conflict-of-interest-at-the-u-s-fish-and-wildlife-service-and-divesting-from-fossil-fuel/

and in later years, especially, many of them treated the Refuge System like their oyster. They traveled incessantly to spectacular refuges, rendezvoused regularly at the National Conservation Training Center, and even jaunted overseas to "assist" foreign nations. Their travelogues would be the envy of National Geographic explorers.

The only lulls in the busy travel schedules of the Refuge System chiefs were at times of intense political scrutiny or fear. These periods included the first few months of new presidencies, especially when George W. Bush and Donald Trump were elected. That's because Republican candidates of recent times have advertised their extreme emphasis on economic growth, coupled with an eagerness to pare back any government programs putting a drag on GDP.[42]

Other periods when the chiefs laid low and stayed out of airports came in the wake of controversial travel incidents such as the $800,000 party thrown by the General Services Administration in 2010 (in Las Vegas, no less). In fact, that's a good segue to the travel habits of the Refuge System chiefs.

The first incident of tax-paid, high-dollar, unseemly travel I recall was a meeting of various Refuge System chiefs on Kodiak Island. You read that right: on Kodiak Island! Not only did these chiefs travel to Alaska from all parts of the country (these were headquarters chiefs plus a few of the regional equivalents); they traveled to an Alaskan island that is notoriously difficult and expensive to get to.

For many readers outside the wildlife profession, this location may not immediately resonate, but wildlifers, hunters, outdoor photographers, and nature tourists will recognize it as iconic. Kodiak Island is the land of huge grizzly bears that congregate at rivers with spectacular runs of salmon. You've probably 'been there' on the Discovery Channel or in the pages of *National Geographic*. For the wildlife professional, going to Kodiak Island is akin to the business professional going to Dubai. It's a far-off location that is so stimulating to members of the profession that merely being there is more like recreation than work.

I don't recall the details of the Kodiak Island meeting, but I do know it drew the ire of staffers in the Washington Office. Everyone knew the Kodiak trip was: 1) extremely expensive, 2) absolutely unnecessary, and 3) a junket designed for the enjoyment of the attendees. Conscientious staffers were appalled, frustrated, and even embarrassed for the Refuge System, which

---

[42] The fear of Republican fiscal conservatism should not be conflated with suppression of the 800-Pound Gorilla, which was a non-partisan pursuit.

shared the building with less fiscally advantaged programs such as Ecological Services (the folks dealing with endangered species listing and recovery), Fisheries and Habitat Conservation, and the National Wetlands Inventory. Yet there were a handful of other staffers, including future branch chiefs, whose primary response was envy. They *aspired* to chiefdom in order to join the Refuge System travel club.

It's not that meetings in Alaska are always unreasonable for Refuge System employees. Alaska has 16 refuges and a regional office in Anchorage. But Anchorage—not Kodiak Island—is precisely where most Alaskan meetings should occur. Those biologists, managers, and planners who really want to see Kodiak Island can then take annual leave and spend their own money on travel and lodging costs entailed by a Kodiak Island visit. Even that type of arrangement is unseemly, because the prospect of having one's travel paid to the jump-off point for a wildlifer's paradise creates a bias toward meetings in gateway cities such as Anchorage, Honolulu, and Tampa.

Devil's advocates (such as Refuge System chiefs) might say, "Czech is treating a highly nuanced issue, full of grey area, as simply black or white." They might argue that the wildlife professional needs an occasional dose of wildlife to stay motivated. Meeting on Kodiak Island, they'd argue, would have positive side effects such as re-charging the spirit of the employee or even teaching them ecological lessons that might come in handy one day.

In turn, I would acknowledge *some* grey area, but it's not the role of the taxpayer to ensure our highest-paid, most fun-having employees are provided yet more perks on the federal dole. If any Refuge System chief so badly needs to be pampered, entertained, or excited, they should be replaced by someone among the thousands of unemployed or re-directed wildlife biologists who come complete with a conservation ethic sturdy enough to sustain their psyches—and their workflow—without paid meetings on Kodiak Island.

The only grey area pertains to the taking of leave—let's say for that trip to Kodiak Island—before or after a legitimate meeting in a city such as Anchorage. Even then it offends the senses to think that taxpayers should be paying for travel to the gateway city, lodging therein, and a generous allotment of per diem as the chief gets ready to "let 'er rip." It just doesn't pass the smell test. Therefore, the unwritten rule should be, "Just don't do it."

Then there's the bias toward "face-time" meetings (as opposed to teleconferences and webinars) due to the draw of *non*-wildlife entertainment. Meetings in San Diego, New Orleans, Seattle, Washington, DC and a long list of other fun, historic, or otherwise vacation-worthy cities are far more common than warranted by the duties and projects of Refuge System personnel. While not as gaudily abusive as a Kodiak Island trip, meetings at these destinations are very expensive, given the lodging costs and per-diem rates.

Per diem may not be well-known to the taxpayer, but it should be. "Per diem" literally means "for each day" in Latin, but the phrase is used by federal employees as shorthand for the compensation they receive for lodging, meals, and "incidental" expenses. Per diem for meals, in particular, is given to the employee whether or not the expenses are truly incurred.

Whether for lodging, meals, or incidental expenses, per-diem rates are generous—very generous—and they vary by region and city. For example, the chief who travels to New Orleans for a winter meeting will receive $236 per day in per diem, with no questions asked. It doesn't matter if the chief gorges on gateau at Gautreau's or grabs some grub at Grandy's. Nor does it matter if the chief gets a free breakfast at the hotel, goes out to a fancy brunch, or simply skips breakfast. No matter, either, if a professor or a mayor or national wildlife refuge "friends group" hosts the employee at dinner for three days straight... $236 per day is added to that employee's paycheck.

I once saw a Refuge System chief exclaim to a staffer planning a long trip to Africa—yes, Africa—"That's going to be a huge per-diem check!" Her eyes were wide, she sounded positively awed, and there was no laughter or chuckling to indicate a sardonic joke. I was astounded, as I'd never seen her that animated about her actual duties.

The untoward fact is that Refuge System chiefs are *notorious* for collecting gaudy amounts of per diem due to their frequency of travel and selection of expensive meeting destinations. Toward the end of my FWS career I coined a phrase to describe this phenomenon: "per-diem bonus." Incessant travelers such as Geoff Pudert, Cynthia Martinis, and Arun Lyze were masters of the per-diem bonus. Not that they didn't receive other types of Bible Club bonuses, but the per-diem bonus was the most systematically and subtly corrupt. Their annual income was boosted by hundreds or even thousands of dollars, *purely from per diem*.

Even without the per-diem bonus, these were no professionally persecuted, financially struggling civil servants. Most if not all of the chiefs I've noted were among the 100 top-paid employees of the entire FWS.[43]

To add insult to injury, these gag-ordering per-diem masters provided paper-thin rationale for their excessive travel. Who from Refuge System headquarters could forget the embarrassing "newsletter" from Cynthia Martinis,

---

[43] See https://www.federalpay.org/employees/us-fish-and-wildlife-service/top-100.

circa 2017, when she wrote, "The Refuge System life can be a travelling life," and had the gall to send it to all Refuge System employees. She went on to describe some of her recent travels, making them sound like they were all about conservation—almost like a sacrifice—while staffers hypothesized her habit of travelling back and forth to her home state of New Mexico was largely for the free travel for visiting family and friends.[44]

Possibly the king of the per-diem bonus was Pudert. He constantly travelled all over the United States—plus numerous trips around the world—drawing the ire of administrative personnel who spent half their time assisting him with travel plans. It seemed like the other half of their time was spent processing receipts—and per-diem payments—from past travel.

Pudert also gets credit for the only statement to rival Martinis's "travelling life" embarrassment. He muttered it in a tiny branch meeting one day toward the end of my time at headquarters. I suspect he came up with it for my benefit, because he was probably aware of my budding interest in the travel habits of the chiefs. He was reporting in droll fashion on his long list of meetings from a long list of places. Amidst copious "ah, ah, ah" utterances, he managed to nervously aver (and I paraphrase), "The one thing I've learned is that, ah, ah, to make things happen, um, you have to be there." I remember thinking, "Nothing's going to happen anywhere with *that* kind of enunciation."

Lyze, meanwhile, didn't take long to develop a reputation for back-and-forth trips to Colorado. The regional office in Denver, plus offices in Fort Collins and a handful of national wildlife refuges, provided convenient drop-offs for family visits and hunting trips.

It's not entirely fair to pick on Martinis, Pudert, and Lyze. Not when virtually the entire collection of Refuge System chiefs were notorious for incessant travel, combining it with vacations, and supplementing their income with the per-diem bonus. Most of the staffers, on the other hand, did no such thing, and most of them wouldn't have, even if given the chance. There were some true-blue conservationists among the staff who resisted travel unless it was absolutely necessary. When they did have to travel, they would assist our administrative staff in finding reasonable prices on transportation and lodging.

This attitude alone—pertaining to travel—was something that separated the Bible Club from the rest. The Bible Club hid behind the commendable

---

[44] Unfortunately for Martinis, the "traveling life" may have hit a dead end circa 2021, when she was evidently put on paid administrative leave for driving under the influence.

mission of the Refuge System and fooled themselves into thinking that, because they were working for the Refuge System, they were conservationists.

Ironically, I cannot provide the reader with names, dates, destinations, and per-diem dollars accruing to Refuge System chiefs, because I was threatened with an "investigation" when I attempted to gather some of these data at the end of my career. I could have fought it, but to what avail? The "disciplinary actions" they'd piled on me over the years meant that any benefit of doubt would be used to tan my hide and toss it out the door. Meanwhile, being under "investigation," I was never going to see the data anyway.

After I quit, perhaps I could have issued a request, pursuant to the Freedom of Information Act, for the travel data information. However, having worked on some FOIA requests, I knew exactly how the Refuge System would stall, object, and attempt to level a hefty fee for procuring the information. Again, I was unlikely to ever receive the data, so I decided it wasn't worth the hassle, especially given the heavy lift of rebuilding CASSE.

Taxpayers should know, however, that the Refuge System chiefs tried to portray the travel data as "personal records." Personal records are documents pertaining to the likes of social security accounting, health history, and beneficiary identification, and they are not to be shared with the public or even within the agency (with limited exceptions, such as among human resources staff). Yet calling the travel data "personal records" was bogus—an outright lie, actually—and designed for only two purposes: to prevent an inspection of their wanton travel behavior, and to accuse me of malfeasance or some other generic charge.

I tracked down the agency's own list of types of personal records and showed it to them. Nothing on the list was remotely related to travel records. The chief they'd put in charge of the "investigation" simply reacted, "Well they are now."

The system was rigged, in other words. I wasn't going to get the data, so I left them with their travel records, went on to manage CASSE, and eventually finished the expose you hold in your hands. Soon afterward I was told the chiefs got busy expunging old travel records; to what degree and how far back is anyone's guess.

That said, the concerned taxpayer, conservation organization, or government watchdog can always issue a FOIA request for the travel records of Refuge System chiefs (especially at headquarters), including names, dates, expenditures, etc. If the requester is not going to use the information for commercial purposes, FWS is required to provide it, essentially free of charge.

If the requester happens to be a membership or watchdog organization such as PEER, FWS won't get away with suppression tactics as easily as when a FOIA request is made by an individual citizen.

Meanwhile, let's consider a few more examples of Refuge System boondoggles and per-diem abuses.

The Refuge System has a research vessel called the *Tiglax* that ports in Homer, Alaska. What Kodiak Island is to grizzly bears—and grizzly bear watchers—Homer is to halibut and halibut fishermen. The *Tiglax*, pronounced Tech'-la (Aleut for eagle) is used primarily for the study of marine and coastal ecology on and around the Alaska Maritime National Wildlife Refuge.

At least the taxpayer would *hope* the *Tiglax* is used primarily for research. All we know for sure is that she's been used for much more than that.

Some time around the year 2014, an up-and-coming headquarters staffer named Ryan Slayem spent several weeks on the *Tiglax*. Slayem was more respectable than most of the chiefs; he was a serious, productive employee at headquarters. Yet no dataset or research report was ever circulated pursuant to Slayem's trip on the *Tiglax*, much less used for any legitimate management purposes, and certainly not published for broader scientific use or public information.

Among Refuge System staff, Slayem's trip was thought to be a boondoggle; in particular a sort of reward, perhaps for performance, or perhaps for fealty to the Bible Club. Surely the Bible Club would proffer phrases such as "reconnaissance" or "management planning," but even more surely there was sightseeing, birdwatching, whale-watching, and most likely some fishing.

Slayem was far from the only part-time sailor with the Refuge System. Sean Sanchez, the "deputy chief" (and old buddy of Cynthia Martinis), spent weeks aboard the *Tiglax* and had so much fun he wrote something of a travelogue for the benefit of Refuge System staff.

I strongly suspect that most—maybe not all—the Refuge System chiefs have done some "living on *Tiglax* time." Most likely with plenty of beer, fishing, and general sightseeing on the way to and from Homer. Those who haven't would seem to prefer other Refuge System vacationing prospects. As Martinis would say, "The Refuge System life can be a travelling life."

Taxpayers should know one more thing about the *Tiglax*. The per-diem rate for Homer, Alaska is approximately $253, including approximately $124 for meals. Talk about eating high off the halibut!

Then there was the 2015 trip to Paris for COP21, the Conference of the Parties at which the "Paris Climate Accords" were drawn up. At least a dozen

Refuge System chiefs and aspiring chiefs from the Bible Club happily spent a week in "gay Paris," eating *foie gras*, drinking wine and beer and spirits, and generally seeing the sights. After all, not a single one of them was there to take part in the negotiations.

For me, the Bible Club's collective Paris boondoggle added more insult to injury than other boondoggles to Alaska, Hawaii, Florida, Maine, California, Canada, Mexico, Puerto Rico, Guam, Russia, China, or Africa. As the de facto climate change coordinator, I was the one most suited to productive participation at COP21 and its satellite meetings and symposia. I would have shared information on running the SLAMM model and the implications of our modeling to international migratory bird conservation. I could have garnered information for use in the climate change primer. I would have developed long-lasting collegial networks helpful for Refuge System planning in the coming years.

Instead, taxpayers sent travel-club card carriers who didn't know SLAMM from ham de paris, before or after COP21. We (taxpayers) paid close to $100,000 (2023 dollars) to do so. And what did we get in return? Don't ask me. Don't ask any of the FWS staffers who toiled away at headquarters while the Bible Club was carrying on in Paris, either. We have no idea. We saw no results.

Now, there was at least one fellow who must have *chatted* a lot about climate change. Despite having done no work in climate change, one John Smerfield had been recently selected for the paid, GS-14 version of the Climate Change Coordinator position (as opposed to the de facto position I'd occupied in tandem with my GS-13 conservation biologist position). I dutifully passed the baton with copious climate files upon Smerfield's coronation to the prized, non-supervisory yet "management team" position.

Smerfield had a patently non-distinctive persona and seemed to slide through his high-paid duties without producing anything except his half of never-ending conversations. As the supervisor of another, non-refuge program asked on several occasions, "Does that guy ever *do* anything?" Dirth called him "Smurf" after the soft, harmless, and relatively irrelevant cartoon characters. (Dirth was nothing if not reckless with his nicknaming.)

Very early in Smerfield's stint as Climate Change Coordinator, we drove out to a meeting in Annapolis, Maryland. It was an interagency meeting about sea-level rise modeling and planning for the Chesapeake Bay. Smerfield was communicative and seemed like a fairly nice fellow, so I decided to tell him the basics about my experience with the 800-Pound Gorilla at Refuge

System headquarters. I concluded with something to the effect of, "I'm not saying we should be out there demonstrating on the White House lawn, but we should be carefully developing a systematic approach to raising awareness of the trade-off between economic growth and wildlife conservation."

Smerfield replied, with as much emphasis as I'd ever hear him muster, "I absolutely agree with you, 100 percent," and even went on to elaborate to some degree. I won't say I was surprised, because anyone with half a conservation brain would agree that we should indeed be developing precisely such an approach. Anyone outside the Bible Club, at least. The Bible Club just happened to be exceedingly unique—or at least exceedingly extreme—in pitting itself against the realities of ecological economics.

While I wasn't surprised, I was certainly appreciative. It felt refreshing and gratifying to suddenly have someone of higher rank at Refuge System headquarters express their support for the obvious, even if they'd taken a job I was more qualified for.

Alas, Smerfield was merely months away from donning the comforting cottons of his Smurf smock in the shadow of the 800-Pound Gorilla. We were at a two-day "retreat" across the Potomac River in Washington, DC, shuttling back and forth on the DC Metro trains. There were no fancy hotels for this one. (When staffers were involved, travel perks were not so pronounced.) We were there along with the rest of the Division of Natural Resources and Conservation Planning, and Dirth made one of his obligatory "leadership" appearances to apprise us of the state of the budget and whatever vision he had for programmatic priorities. In typical gratuitous fashion, he "opened the floor" for "completely open" questions and concerns, with "nothing off the table."

Anyone with my combination of education and experience would have been virtually obligated to note that, while we might be winning some conservation battles here and there, we were being routed in the war. Our only chance to prevail for wildlife conservation in the long run was to stabilize the size of the human economy. While we obviously couldn't formulate the nation's economic policies, we just as obviously had the unique obligation to raise public awareness of the trade-off between economic growth and wildlife conservation. If we didn't do it, I asked, who else would?

I also pointed out that I'd been told for over a decade by Refuge System leadership that I was simply ahead of my time, that truly we would one day have to weigh in on the 800-Pound Gorilla. I asked Dirth if he thought now (roughly 2013) was finally the time, at least for some baby steps in raising awareness. I felt I could count on certain staffers and at least one program leader—Mr. John Smerfield, Climate Change Coordinator—to back me up.

Unfortunately, it was almost noon, and the timing was no coincidence. Dirth could always expect to be saved by the bell, with the tough topics evaded, if the "open floor" threatened to interfere with lunch and a midday beer for the Bible Club. And so it was like clockwork when Dirth trotted out the tired excuse that "it's not our role" and called it a morning, summarily dismissing any discussion of the 800-Pound Gorilla.

Dirth's paper-thin consideration of the topic was no surprise, and neither was the timing, but there was a modicum of chance to turn the timing in our favor ("our" meaning the real conservationists among the staff, presumably including Smerfield). We could let the attendees reflect during lunch upon the 800-Pound Gorilla, as well as Dirth's flippant dismissal, and perhaps get it back into the discussion while attendees were re-assembling for the afternoon sessions.

In fact, this prospect was palpable in the minutes leading up to the afternoon session. Most of us were back at the meeting tables, which were arranged in one big square. Dirth was there, having stuck around for the afternoon's opening session. So, I sidled up to Smerfield, the GS-14 Climate Change Coordinator who had "absolutely" agreed with me about the FWS role in raising awareness of the trade-off between economic growth and wildlife conservation, and asked, "John, what do you think about raising awareness of the trade-off between economic growth and wildlife conservation? You think we should try to get that back on the table?" While he wasn't in control of the afternoon agenda, he had enough influence to get the issue back on the table.

To my utter dismay and disgust, "Smurf" glanced over at Dirth, looked back toward me, and announced, "I agree with Jim. It's not our role to be talking about economic growth." My immediate thought was, "What the hell?"

Smerfield had become a yes-man in near-record time. He was now to Dirth what Dirth was to Crasche. He was less concerned with doing the right thing, the effective thing, the necessary thing for conservation, than he was with pleasing his Bible Club master, solidifying the newest rung on his career ladder, and preparing for his proverbial (and literal) Paris trips.

While the trip to Paris was particularly galling to me—the civil servant who had built the climate change program from scratch—the trips that would probably most gall the taxpayer were the ones to China. The details of these trips were kept from public and even FWS staffer view. I believe many of the partakers would have gleefully gone without ever telling a soul if they could have gotten away with it, because everyone knew these trips would never pass a government accountability smell test. As one staffer closer than I to the management team described it, the cumulative Chinese trip (taken by just about every member of the management team, and multiple times by several) was "100 percent boondoggle, no products ever; purely a paid vacation."

The disgusting examples could go on and on. An entire galling opus could be produced on this topic alone—The *Idiads and Their Odysseys* comes to mind—but the point is this: Refuge System chiefs abused their travel privileges to a fiscally obscene degree. They lost all claim to the title "conservationist," or even "civil servant." They essentially committed shades of petty crime in the gray areas between "innocent" joy-riding and outright embezzlement. The ugliest part is, they not only took tax-paid dollars for their entertainment, but they diverted these funds from bona fide, civilly-serving conservation efforts.

Think for a moment about the millions of dollars—yes *millions*—spent over the decades by Refuge System chiefs on unnecessary meetings, associated joy-riding, and outright boondoggles. Now imagine the same millions going into the careful planning and execution of a program for raising public awareness of the trade-off between growth and conservation. Would we still have virtually no public dialog on limits to growth? No media coverage? No "steady state economy" in the vernacular?

While we'll never know precisely how much dialog or policy reform we may have produced, one thing is certain: There was no chance for any of it for the *two decades* of my career, as Refuge System chiefs chose sightseeing over steady statesmanship.

Although the anecdotes above appear in past tense, sightseeing behavior among the Refuge System chiefs surely didn't evaporate upon my resignation. Ironically, though, unjustified travel by cabinet-level appointees provided FWS leadership with some political cover during the Trump Administration. Trump's first Secretary of the Interior, Ryan Zinke, along with EPA Administrator Scott Pruitt, were notorious for racking up the mileage and living high off the hog (or halibut), empowered by Trump's own profligate behavior and his notorious lack of a conservation ethic.

At the time of this writing (October 2023) it's evidently different in the Biden Administration, with Deb Haaland as Secretary of the Interior. However, the problem is far from gone for good. Whether under a supportive administration (such as the Obama Administration) or a profligate-in-its-own-right administration (such as Trump's), Refuge System chiefs have proven to be like kids in a candy shop, with nobody minding the bins.

Fortunately, reforming the Refuge System, FWS, DOI, and government travel at large is not rocket science. In-person, national-level meetings should be held in locations such as St. Louis, Indianapolis, and Oklahoma City. These are geographically centralized locations and hubs for major airlines. Rumor has it that the tables, chairs, cell towers, and wifi connections in these cities are every bit as functional as the ones in Anchorage or Honolulu. Food and lodging costs are modest, and the chambers of commerce do their best to welcome travelers on business.

Obviously, meetings with a more regional focus should be held in regional counterparts that offer such geographic and economic efficiency. In many cases, regional meetings *are* held in such efficient locations, partly because these locations correspond with regional offices. Examples include Minneapolis, Atlanta, and Denver. Each hosts a regional FWS office, a major airline hub, and reasonably priced lodging.

Privileged chiefs in all agencies, but especially in the FWS and Refuge System, need a reminder of what it means to be a leader. Theodore Roosevelt said, "Nothing in the world is worth having or worth doing unless it means effort, pain, and difficulty." He didn't mean the "effort" of airline travel, the "pain" of per-diem paperwork, or the "difficulty" in skirting a challenge. In the FWS, leadership at the national level means identifying the biggest challenges to wildlife conservation, then mustering the fortitude to address precisely those challenges.

11

"DUMBING IT DOWN"

IS CONDUCIVE TO DUMMIES

Federal agencies are required to put things in "plain language" pursuant to the Plain Writing Act of 2010 and President Obama's Executive Order 13563. The logic is simple and obvious: Taxpayers should be able to understand what their taxes are being used for.

The plain-language guidelines apply to federal scientists as much as anyone else in the civil service, or even more so. Government scientists are constantly challenged to express complex scientific principles and findings on topics that, in some cases, are exceedingly important to the future of the country, its citizens, and even the planet. Topics that come to mind are climate change, biodiversity loss, and limits to growth.

"Dumbing it down," as the plain-language requirement is cynically referred to in the bureaucracy, is a difficult, underappreciated balancing act between scientific rigor and public communication. It's a balancing act while threading a needle. The government scientist must take a convoluted ball of yarn and distill its contents into pithy, resonant messages to get through the eye of the needle into public understanding. The eye of the needle, meanwhile, is a moving target controlled by government editors, chiefs, and political appointees.

Although I've had issues with the eye of the needle, I've always agreed with the spirit of the plain-language mandate. Long before I signed on with FWS, I saw the need for translating ecological and economic principles for the "lay" audience. I didn't grow up in an ivory tower, and never forgot where I came from. Having worked in a packing plant in Wisconsin, on ranches out West, and construction in Texas, I could talk shop with "the base."

What I never came to appreciate, however, was the amount of dumbing down required *within* FWS; in particular the dumbing down of documents for chiefs' consumption.

Dumbing down for the chiefs should not have been necessary, because there was a long list of unemployed Ph.D. graduates (and untold masters graduates) in the wildlife profession. Meanwhile there were Refuge System chiefs who actually *boasted* of landing their positions without any graduate degree! Such boasting was disgusting to me, because virtually every one of the Ph.D. students I came to know at the universities of Wisconsin, Washington, and Arizona were better qualified than the majority of chiefs at headquarters. These students were representative of the 106 land-grant colleges and universities across the country, and most of them could have run conservation circles around the chiefs.

One day circa 2011 I was in the office of Debra Pock, the division chief who'd recently issued me a gag order and was now reprimanding me for raising the issue of the 800-Pound Gorilla (which I had, but only barely, confined to her office and in tip-toe fashion). Her upbraiding was surreal because, not only was she on board with ecological economics, but she was a CASSE signatory! She had signed the CASSE position on economic growth, acknowledging the fundamental conflict between economic growth and biodiversity conservation, before ever accepting her position at headquarters.[45]

Yet here we were, in her office, and she was laying down the law. Bible Club law. While it was frustrating to me, even *she* seemed oddly flustered by the whole scenario. I'd only gingerly noted the 800-Pound Gorilla—I think the context was land acquisition planning—and Pock was finding it difficult to specify precisely what I'd done wrong. She finally acknowledged, "I don't know anything about this topic," and that she'd have to defer to me on the particulars.[46]

Then the discussion turned toward how a wildlife biologist ever lands on such a topic to begin with. I summarized for Pock how my work experience and conservation research had led me to ecological economics. I told her I'd studied 81 credits worth of Ph.D. curriculum at the University of Arizona. I wanted to point out to her (as I did to readers in Chapter 1) that I was a serious student, and I was clearly on the defensive, so I mentioned my 4.0 GPA. Given Pock's confusion and indecisiveness about dealing with the

---

[45] The CASSE position on economic growth is online at www.steadystate.org.

[46] For a summary of the relevance of economic growth to conservation land-acquisition strategy and planning, see: Czech, B. 2002. A transdisciplinary approach to conservation land acquisition. *Conservation Biology* 16(6):1488-1497.

800-Pound Gorilla, I felt she would need every bit of rationale she could muster, if she were ever to push back on the Bible Club suppression. I assumed my bona fides would be helpful in that regard.

So, it felt like the backfire of a cheap dirt bike when Pock's knee-jerk response was, "So what?" Not only was I once again stopped in my tracks by a petty branch chief, I was taken aback, because Pock was one of the rare Refuge System bureaucrats (rare at headquarters) who also had a Ph.D. I thought she'd have some appreciation for the diligence my curriculum entailed.

In retrospect, I shouldn't have been surprised. The subject of her own Ph.D. had been narrower than a pintail's hinder. She'd analyzed isotopes from the feathers of a few migratory bird species with wintering grounds on different continents. She wanted to find if the feathers grown on different continents had different stable isotope ratios. It was an obscure, esoteric study of laboratory methods that bore as much fruit as a fig tree in Finland.

(I had to wonder what Dick Schultz would have thought.)

Despite the Ph.D. and the esoteric nature of her research, Pock became a good example of the disturbing tendency in the FWS to dumb it down, way down. It was as if dumbing it down was some type of noble endeavor that would bring us straight to the political center of the American public, and as if reaching that center was the mission of the agency, rather than the conservation of fish and wildlife for present and future generations of Americans.

The Dumb-It-Down Syndrome, or "DIDS" (for acronym-appreciating bureaucrats), is prominent, problematic, and important enough to warrant a chapter. It greatly contributed to the propensity of Refuge System "leaders" to issue gag orders on topics beyond their levels of academic accomplishment. DIDS haunted me from my first year in the Refuge System to my last. I'll summarize just two examples, both pertaining to land conservation strategy.

In my first year with the Refuge System, I served on the Land Acquisition Priority System (LAPS) team. I found LAPS to be an extremely primitive system for ranking lands for acquisition. The basic approach was, if the project would protect a species that had in some way been recognized as important (such as migratory birds, threatened and endangered species, or marine mammals), the project would be awarded a few more points. Such equivalence of apples to oranges was of great interest to me, because a significant element of my Ph.D. curriculum was an assessment of the relative merits—conservation and political merits—of species.

In particular, I had developed the argument that species should be prioritized using the metaphor of the burning library. The fireman entering the library would conduct a sort of literary triage. Let's start with what the literary fireman would be *least* likely to prioritize. It requires only a modicum of common sense to think of examples such as comic books, newsletters, and the serial joke sheets that appear in homespun restaurants. These types of documents contain tiny bits of information, the vast majority of which is hardly important to the literature at large. Perhaps just as importantly, they took (or should have taken) minimal time to produce, written literally overnight in many cases. In other words, few resources were invested in their production, and not much was to be gained from their consumption.

Such documents would tend to exhibit little distinctiveness, either. For every comic book on the rack, many others contain the same basic themes and plotlines, with only slight differences in the details and variations.

At the other end of the spectrum (or, actually, the three spectra alluded to), we would find the epic tomes of antiquity. *On the Revolutions of the Celestial Spheres*, *The Fabric of the Human Body*, and *The Principia* took decades of determined toil and profound thought to produce. In other words, substantial resources were allocated to their production. Copernicus, Vesalius, and Newton, respectively, packed these tomes with invaluable information. They contain chapters, sections, and even volumes and editions of material that cover tremendous philosophical and scientific territory. Our additional criterion of distinctiveness finds its pinnacle with such classics, too. We all have a far better chance of reproducing a joke sheet than *The Principia*.

And so it is with the likes of grizzly bears, California condors, and alligators. These species were millions of years in the evolutionary making, are replete with form and function, and have no equals in the economy of nature.

Of course, at some point we must graduate from metaphor and put our principles into technical terms that reflect their scientific merits and measurability. These terms happen to be "functional genome size," "niche breadth," and "molecular clock speed." Species of high functional genome size (copious DNA minus "junk DNA"), broad niches, and slow molecular clock (mutation rate) are like the tomes of antiquity in the library. It so happens a sort of litmus test for qualifying as a tome is…a backbone.

Vertebrates, in other words, warrant more conservation attention than invertebrates. They are the tomes of evolutionary antiquity. Species of flies, on the other hand, are more like evolutionary flashes in the pan. They come and go quickly, almost like individual flies. If a fly species blinks out, another one can quickly—relatively speaking—evolve back into the vacated niche. It can be "authored" right back into the "library," especially given the faster mutation rates of invertebrates.

Luckily, with the distinction between vertebrates and invertebrates, politics were on our side for a change. Congress itself had prioritized vertebrates over invertebrates in authorizing the listing of "distinct populations" of vertebrates—but not invertebrates—as "species" pursuant to the Endangered Species Act. Now I was bringing the technical rationale for prioritizing vertebrates to the Land Acquisition Priority System. It wouldn't have required a tremendous amount of complexity, either. Land acquisition projects designed to conserve vertebrate species would have simply ranked higher than projects designed to conserve invertebrates. The only issue to settle was: How much higher?

When I presented my thesis in a plenary session of the North American Wildlife and Natural Resources Conference, the audience was full of knowing nods and appreciative approval. Yet when I layed it out for the LAPS team, I was met with blank stares. Only one fellow seemed able to engage at all, but even his input was to the effect, "There's just no way we can deal with this level of complexity in LAPS." My proposal was summarily dismissed, and we kept on giving just as many LAPS points for conserving naucorids and wallflowers as red wolves and whooping cranes.

That's DIDS.

Perhaps the most costly case of DIDS occurred closer to 2005. Again the general topic was land acquisition, so some of the "DIDers" remained from the old LAPS team. The topic should have been much easier to handle, though. The topic was optimizing our land acquisition expenditures.

It doesn't take an economics degree—not even a one-credit course at a community college—to recognize that the merits of a purchase are determined by what you get and how much you pay. As any ol' trucker knows, you're after the "biggest bang for the buck." The hardly intimidating term used to describe this concept in economics is "benefit:cost analysis." Yet, in all the years I served at headquarters, Refuge System chiefs obstinately refused to conduct it!

Nothing could have been simpler, either. LAPS already produced a ranking of land acquisition projects based on the ecological merits of the lands in question. The maximum LAPS score was 800 (plus 50 for meeting some simple administrative criteria). Two hundred points were available for benefits to migratory bird benefits, 200 more for fisheries and aquatic resources, 200 for threatened and endangered species, and a final 200 for "ecosystem conservation" (a component I *was* able to get installed, with points going to the conservation of under-represented ecosystems). If a land acquisition project could accomplish a fair bit of everything above, it could score well into the 700+ range.

Now what if you had two such projects, with one of them costing a million dollars an acre, and the other costing a thousand dollars an acre?

Surely no one with a lick of sense would fail to recognize the better deal. And, to give the Refuge System chiefs the tiny bit of credit due, they argued that ridiculous rip-offs would be spotted, and the Director would overrule LAPS and ensure that such projects weren't approved.

Yet rip-offs *were* approved, such as extremely expensive "postage stamps" on the Florida coast: tiny parcels that were, to make matters worse, highly vulnerable to sea-level rise. But that's not even the main point here; not the cardinal sin. The real issue is that a simple dividing of LAPS score by price per acre would have systematically, substantially increased the conservation benefits of each and every year's allocation of land acquisition money. It was by far *the* most obvious way to optimize our use of the Land and Water Conservation Fund, our primary funding source for land acquisition.

Yet again, it wasn't rocket science to understand the principle, but the resistance was so strong that I had to conduct a detailed analysis, with the help of a University of Maryland intern. We showed beyond any doubt, with quantifiable examples, the increase in conservation by accounting for costs as well as benefits.

Even then, the Refuge System chiefs refused to adopt this straightforward mechanism for optimizing taxpayer dollars, complaining that it unnecessarily complicated the land acquisition process. It was a bogus complaint, because estimated land prices were already a requirement of land conservation proposals! The complaint begged the question, why bother gathering such information if it wasn't to be used? Yes, the land-price estimates were sometimes rough, but no rougher than the LAPS scores, which didn't even distinguish betweeen vertebrates and invertebrates.

That's DIDS on steroids, and it nearly resulted in a "waste, fraud, and abuse" complaint at the Office of Inspector General. (It would have, but the Land and Water Conservation Fund didn't meet the monetary threshold.)

12

TRUE CONSERVATION:

A VISION WORTHY OF A DIRECTOR

The 21st century challenges to wildlife conservation are unprecedented. The ecological integrity of the nation and planet is unravelling before our eyes. Species and ecosystems are disappearing, if not immediately off the face of the planet, then via slow, dead-end emigrations away from warming climes as they respond to climate change.

It's not as if climate change was needed to imperil fish and wildlife. Climate change is actually the fourth major crisis in the past 150 years. First was the overhunting that extinguished species like the passenger pigeon and extirpated many others from much of their range (bison, for example). Next was habitat loss: the degradation, destruction, and wholesale replacement of habitats in every state. Think, for example, of the Florida panther or the San Joaquin kit fox. Third, intimately interlinked with the second, was the pollution of air, soil, and water, most dramatically represented by the buildup of DDT that nearly extinguished the bald Eagle, peregrine falcon, and other symbols of the American wilds.

And now, due to the greenhouse gases emitted by a $100 trillion global economy (driven significantly by the $20 trillion American economy) we have climate change; perhaps more aptly labeled "global heating." Actually, climate change has been impacting wildlife populations for decades, but we are just starting to realize how ubiquitous and devastating the effects are.

Furthermore, the habitat and pollution crises are far from over. While the growth of the economy has slowed in recent years, it's not for lack of intent or pro-growth policy. Economic growth remains the overriding domestic policy goal of the United States as well as an American priority in international affairs. As long as this holds, wildlife will be increasingly imperiled and extinguished as habitats are lost and polluted.

Finally, no one should assume the overhunting problem has been solved forever. As the economy outstrips its long-term capacity, society faces a 21st century struggle for subsistence. Widespread poverty will bring more intensive hunting and fishing, liberalization of game laws, and ultimately poaching.

Much has already been lost, but priceless populations and species of wildlife hang in the balance. American taxpayers are counting on the U.S. Fish and Wildlife Service to lead the way in protecting our wildlife heritage. Who else would they expect to do the job?

The problem is, the agency has lost its way. That's my opinion, after nearly two decades at FWS headquarters. Inconvenient truths have been shrouded for the sake of perks and pleasures among the higher ranks. No one person is going to fix the FWS, yet some individuals are especially important to the future of the agency. None is more important than the Director.

Herein, I propose a vision that the 21st century FWS Director will need in order to be effective. I'll call it "True Conservation."

Professional Background, Personality, and Priorities

A vision of True Conservation isn't possible without certain intellectual prerequisites. That's not a reference to intelligence; that trait should go without saying. Rather, I'm referring to a mastery of particular fields of knowledge. For starters, the Director must be an expert in wildlife biology and ecosystem ecology. An FWS Director without such mastery is like an Attorney General without a law degree or a Treasury Secretary without an economics education. Given the glut of wildlife biologists, many of whom have given up on careers due to lack of opportunities, a bare minimum of a master's degree should be required.

Yet expertise in wildlife science is far from sufficient in the 21st century for True Conservation. An effective Director must be an expert on the *threats* to wildlife. Otherwise, how will they know what to fix and how to fix it? A busy stint as director, which will come and go in a flash, is no time for figuring it out. The Director must come in especially with a solid grasp on the fundamental conflict between economic growth and wildlife conservation. She or he (hereafter, "they"), in other words, must have a solid background in ecological economics; in particular ecological macroeconomics.

Passion is another prerequisite, but it has to originate for the right reasons and apply to the right things. Let us not mistake outdoors enthusiasm for conservation passion. It's not enough to be a passionate hunter, fisher, or birdwatcher, or a passionate defender of the North American Model of Wildlife Conservation. A True Conservation Director will be willing to sacrifice fun times in the field in order to conduce the political, policy, and cultural changes required to slow the runaway train of economic growth. A vision short of that is High-Paid Fun in the Field, not True Conservation.

The FWS Director must be politically savvy, not for purposes of personal advancement, but rather for deft and timely rhetoric. The 21st century Director needs the ability to subtly undermine or outright refute the catastrophic win-win rhetoric that, "There is no conflict between growing the economy and protecting the environment." The opportunities to refute such rhetoric will come every single day, seven days a week, 365 days a year. They must be taken while the Director has the podium and the position.

True Conservation Themes

The FWS Director will face a panoply of conservation challenges. They must wisely appoint the proper assistants to handle most of these challenges, because the Director must maintain a focus on the big-picture, long-term themes of True Conservation. The most important themes will be a conservation ethic, steady-state economics, land conservation, ecological integrity, protecting the Endangered Species Act, conserving biodiversity, and adapting to global heating.

Wildlife conservation is a pipe dream without a truly widespread American conservation ethic. It is up to the director, as much as any other figure in the federal government, to cultivate such an ethic. This doesn't take a degree in sociology or psychology, much less marketing or advertising. (The latter, especially, would be cynically ironic.) Rather, it requires a passionate exposition of the diversity and wonder of our American wildlife, along with the small and simple, everyday practices that conserve our resources and therefore our wildlife.

The Director will have an entire agency as a crucible for cultivating a True Conservation culture. The Director should commence cultivating on Day 1, from their very own office. The lowest-hanging fruit is the light switch. Shutting the lights off will be a message to assistant directors, other staff, and visitors.

It's not enough to talk about Aldo Leopold, leave the lights on, and go eat a steak. If you can't walk the talk, don't walk to the podium.

Conservation practiced in the halls of FWS—starting at the director's office—will emanate to the Department of the Interior, other agencies, and ultimately the American public. After a few months of mastering the messaging in-house, the Director should do all in their power to get the True Conservation message out to the public. This will be within the director's purview, with resources such as the National Conservation Training Center, national wildlife refuge visitor centers, and an entire communications staff at their disposal. "Turn out the lights, use your own mug, and bring your own bag." That's a message all Americans, not just wildlifers, will find relevant, regardless of their interest in wildlife.

The next major theme in True Conservation is steady-state economics. This doesn't mean the Director should, upon the inaugural day for True Conservation, issue a press release renouncing the Full Employment and Balanced Growth Act of 1978. What it means is, from the very start, the Director should be taking baby steps toward correcting the fallacious win-win rhetoric and lengthen those steps throughout their term.

Chances are the Director may never utter the phrase "steady state economy" on television, over the radio, or possibly even before Congress. They can leave a lot of that to the next director. However, the current Director needs to get the ball rolling and cannot abide ignorant notions of "green growth." However subtly the occasion calls for, the Director must interject with pithy lessons on limits to growth, the conflict between growth and conservation, and in some venues, at least, the steady state economy as the sustainable alternative. By now, the Director will find plenty of empowerment in the long list of true conservation giants—Jane Goodall, Sylvia Earle, the late E.O. Wilson and so many others (including past Director Lynn Greenwalt)—who have put their good names to the steady-state mission.

True Conservation absolutely requires land protection. Any FWS Director will have a head start at the helm of the National Wildlife Refuge System: 568 national wildlife refuges encompassing over 800 million acres. Don't be misled by the heady figures, though. The vast majority of acres (over 700 million) are offshore and largely titular, reflecting a political contest during which presidents Bush and Obama "designated" marine conservation areas, but with weak teeth, as GDP-obsessed President Trump quickly demonstrated. Second, of the 95 million terrestrial acres, most are over large expanses of Alaska where little else would have occurred anyway. (Such acreage is cynically referred to in conservation circles as "rock and ice.")

That said, over 20 million acres of national wildlife refuges in the contiguous 48 states are jewels of wildlife conservation, from the tiny Watercress Darter NWR (Alabama) to the sprawling Desert NWR (Nevada). Protecting these refuges will be one of the greatest privileges in the Director's life. They'd better understand the threats.

When the Director thinks about land protection, they should start with one key question: What is a national wildlife refuge a "refuge" from? By now the answer should be clear: the economy. Agriculture, mining, logging, domestic livestock production, commercial fishing, manufacturing, urbanization/services, and the infrastructure that ties it all together such as roads, power lines, and canals; these are what the Director is charged to protect the Refuge System from.

National parks, too, are refuges from the economy, albeit with different purposes. In fact, all units of the conservation estate including national forests, BLM lands, state parks and forests, and county parks are to some degree refuges from the economy. Yes, many of these lands are used for limited economic activities—most notably logging on national forests and cattle grazing on BLM lands—but overall, the economy is precisely what these lands are protected from.

The problem is, refuge lands will be under constant pressure to produce, and not just for outdoor recreation, but the supposed "higher and better" economic uses. The pressure will come directly from the private sector and from other, growth-oriented government agencies, directly and indirectly, as many of these agencies assist the private sector for purposes of GDP growth.

The Director must start making inroads to higher levels of government. The greatest hope for a breakthrough in macroeconomic deliberations at the cabinet level lies with the Secretary of the Interior. Such a breakthrough is highly unlikely unless the Secretary is first informed by, and can subsequently lean on, a knowledgeable FWS Director, who must drive home the point that the FWS mission is undermined by the goal of GDP growth that has permeated the government. The Director will need to recruit allies from within FWS and other Interior agencies in this effort to make the Secretary conversant with the fundamental conflict between economic growth and not only the FWS mission, but much of Interior's collective mission.

Meanwhile, partly as a result of encroaching economic activity, and largely as a result of global heating and other ubiquitous threats (for example, proliferation of "forever chemicals"), the Director will face tricky decisions even on the protected lands of the Refuge System. Pursuant to the Refuge Improvement Act and the ecological integrity policy, the rule of thumb is to manage refuges consistent with natural conditions. This is a philosophical cornerstone, not a cookie-cutter prescription. Exceptions may occur, especially when a refuge was established with other purposes legislated (for example, certain industrial activities at Crab Orchard NWR in Illinois).

Some at FWS have thrown their hands up in the air, correctly acknowledging the game-changing effects of global heating, but incorrectly proclaiming it's game over for the ecological integrity policy. They've based their forfeit on the incorrect impression that the policy requires refuge managers to forever maintain natural conditions. As the lead author of the policy, I know that was never the intent. Rather, the ecological integrity policy simply requires refuge managers to assess what natural conditions were, based upon historic records and the archaeological, anthropological, climatological, and ecological data. All else equal, then, if a management action would take the refuge even further from those natural conditions, it would not be advisable (for example, managing for an artificially high ratio of game:non-game populations). Also, a management action itself can be less natural than others, and therefore less preferable (for example, using herbicides to reduce woody vegetation, rather than prescribed fire).

A chronological frame of reference, such as the one described in Chapter 5, is essential for any comparison of conditions. It helps us to understand that absolute naturalness is no longer possible but is still an ideal to hold to.

An imperfect analogy was given by Vince Lombardi, who said, "Perfection is not attainable, but if we chase perfection we can catch excellence." The Director must hold fast to the concept of ecological integrity, or may otherwise lose control of the Refuge System and watch it turn into a circus of hunting reserves, shooting ranges, zoos, concession stands, and who knows what else for purposes of "stimulating the national economy."[47]

While the Refuge System is important for wildlife conservation, education, and research, refuges are a miniscule fraction of the 48 contiguous states. The director must be a passionate defender of lands, public or private, especially in cases where a species is under imminent threat. This brings us to the next theme of True Conservation, protecting the Endangered Species Act (ESA).

The ESA cannot be understood, much less effective, without an awareness

---

[47] In 2021, then-Deputy Director Martha Williams (confirmed as Director in 2022) called for "stimulating the national economy" by expanding hunting and fishing opportunities on the National Wildlife Refuge System. See https://www.doi.gov/pressreleases/interior-department-announces-largest-expansion-fishing-and-hunting-us-fish-and.

of its economic nexus. It was designed as a collective stop sign. If a project is going to further imperil a federally listed endangered species, it encounters the ESA stop sign. Otherwise, by definition, that species is headed down the road to extinction. Fortunately, the stop signs are easy to see from a distance, and rarely create hardship for well-planned business enterprises.

Unfortunately for wildlife, projects (commercial and public alike) proliferate in lockstep with GDP, many of them are poorly planned, and the causes of species endangerment are like a who's who of the economy. That's why the ESA is nothing less than a prescription—albeit an implicit one—for a steady state economy.

The Director's challenge, then, is not to hide the meaning of ESA and try sneaking it into the political end zone with the win-win rhetoric of "green growth." The challenge starts again with the baby steps of raising awareness—one mind at a time—that in fact we cannot have our cake and eat it too. The ESA is not the enemy. In fact, it is much like a friend, warning us against unsustainable behavior such as gluttony or recklessness. We really ought to cherish this friend, not ignore it, much less gut it in Congress.

The Director with a True Conservation mission will also resist the temptation to emphasize "game" management purely for the pleasure of hunters and fishers. We thought those days were behind us by the time I was hired (1999) as the first "conservation biologist." The principles of conservation biology—most importantly the conservation of biodiversity at large— were behind the Refuge Improvement Act and subsequent FWS visioning exercises such as Fulfilling the Promise and Conserving the Future. Just because one president was so obsessed with GDP growth that the federal agencies were brought to bear for "stimulating the economy"—including ramped up sales of arms, ammunition, and all manner of hunting and fishing gear and activity—doesn't make that shameful episode a legacy to retain. Refuges cannot be treated like another pawn in the chess game of GDP growth. Yes, hunting and fishing is compatible with many of our national wildlife refuges, but on very few refuges (those with legislated exceptions) should it be a top priority. That wouldn't be True Conservation.

Finally, and coming full circle, the 21st century Director must have a cogent response to global heating; that is, a problem-solving approach that addresses the root cause. In the long-term big picture, it just doesn't matter if FWS builds a dike here or rescinds a fire prescription there. The real point for True Conservation is that the Director must help to magnify the staid reports of the Intergovernmental Panel on Climate Change that economic and population growth continue to be the most important drivers of increases in CO_2 emissions."[48]

Institutional Reform

The incoming Director will have plenty of in-house cleanup to do, too, especially at headquarters. Among other things, FWS suffers from poor hiring practices, outdated training priorities, conservation hypocrisy, suppression of science, and the low morale that comes with all the above. None of these problems are intractable. I'll offer just a few ideas for reform, enough to help buttress a True Conservation vision from within the agency.

Given the aforementioned glut of well-qualified wildlife biologists, a graduate degree should be required for biologist and manager positions. (No more boasting by sons of earlier employees that they managed to land a biologist job without a graduate degree.) Merit-based civil service hiring procedures should be strictly applied, and supplemented with additional requirements if necessary, so that a chief can't come into headquarters and summarily hire a staff of drinking buddies from the field. This entails hiring by a committee of peers from other programs, without the involvement or input of an immediate supervisor. Any downsides to this approach are outweighed by the proven penchant for cliquish hiring.

Given the True Conservation themes—conservation ethic, steady-state economics, land conservation, ecological integrity, protecting the ESA, conserving biodiversity, and adapting to global heating—the Director will need to revamp the training curriculum at the National Conservation Training Center (NCTC). Training on the conservation ethic and land conservation are reasonably developed already. The other themes could use some work, and the theme that stands out as in most need of development is steady-state economics.

Given that True Conservation is essentially a steady state economy, FWS seems almost like a sham without a basic understanding of steady-state economics at the staff level, and substantial knowledge of it among the leadership teams. Every FWS employee ought to be conceptually well-equipped to describe the fundamental conflict between economic growth and biodiversity conservation in venues ranging from the elevator to the conference podium. FWS leaders should be able to hold their own in the inevitable debates with economists and "green growth" salesmen, and to

---

[48] See "IPCC Presents Assessment on Measures to Mitigate Climate Change," https://www.unep.org/ru/node/6432.

proffer a vision of steady statesmanship in the Senior Executive Service and potentially at higher levels in the Administration and Congress.

The conservation ethic is taught *about* in some NCTC courses, but that doesn't mean it's taught. That's going to take True Conservation leadership. Meanwhile, "conservation hypocrisy" ranges from leaving the lights on to investing in oil companies via the Thrift Savings Plan. One of the most reprehensible—and most correctable with True Conservation—is the tendency of FWS chiefs to treat their jobs like full-time tourism. There's always an excuse to travel to a refuge for "oversight," a conference for "networking," or even a foreign wildlife agency for "consultation." Yes, some of these events are legitimate, but if a comprehensive travelogue of FWS chiefs were published for the past few decades, it would be scandalous, especially accounting for the per-diem "costs" that are substantially pocketed. Given the carbon footprint of airline travel, the hefty cost to the public, the easy access to online conferencing, and the backlog of duties at the desk, FWS flights (and other government flights) should be phased out, if not by law then by Director's order.

Suppression of science is a nefarious phenomenon. Not only is truth and reality hidden from the taxpaying public but, to put a slight twist on Donald Rumsfeld's lament, we don't know what we don't know. By the very nature of a gag order, we can never really know how many government employees have been gagged, on what topics, for how long, or why. It's a slippery slope, shutting up an employee or shutting down a topic. Every scenario is different, but in True Conservation, an FWS Director doesn't gag a biologist for raising awareness of the trade-off between economic growth and wildlife conservation. If ecological macroeconomics is a strong suit of the employee, the Director recognizes the value and cultivates it rather than snuffing it out. They consult with the employee and either incorporate the knowledge into FWS programs, bring it to the attention of the Secretary, or (if the Director is politically vulnerable) work out an assignment for the employee in a more politically durable agency such as the State Department.

Although there would have been exceptions among a "hook-and-bullet" cohort, FWS morale probably reached an all-time low at FWS during the Trump Administration. (It hadn't been very high since 2014, when most headquarters staff were moved to cubicles in Falls Church, Virginia.) The COVID pandemic didn't help, because it kept a lot of already-insecure staff further in the dark, and the widespread practice of telework has probably postponed any cultural recovery.

Furthermore, I believe that each of the institutional shortcomings noted above, plus of course the sweeping sociopolitical challenges to ecological integrity, have discouraged the majority of FWS employees. Morale must have reached rock bottom when Aurelia Skipwith, Trump's FWS Director, told employees in an all-hands meeting that she'd gone back to law school after being constrained by the law while working for Monsanto.[49]

If future directors lead strongly on the themes of True Conservation and fix the antiquated, corrupting institutional problems at headquarters, morale will soar! Practicing as well as preaching conservation will garner respect. Steady-state economics—with only the basics required for staffers—will refresh a workforce that otherwise faces a growing sense of futility. Not giving up on ecological integrity will assure employees that they're working for the long term, not just a generation or two of hunters and fishers.

Finally, extinguishing the win-win, no-conflict rhetoric will boost morale by excising the cancerous tumor of conservation cynicism. Yes, there most certainly is a conflict between growing the economy and conserving wildlife. The Wildlife Society, U.S. Society for Ecological Economics, American Society of Mammalogists, the late E.O. Wilson, Jane Goodall, Lynn Greenwalt, and many other True Conservation leaders have acknowledged and explicated the conflict. It's long overdue for FWS, the Department of the Interior, and the civil service at large to do likewise.

---

[49] Skipwith's statement from the all-hands meeting was described by a staffer who was present at the meeting. For more on the back-story of Skipwith's ties to industry, see "Ties Exposed Between Westlands Water W.D. [sic; should be "Westlands W.D." for Westlands Water District] and Aurelia Skipwith, Trump's Nominee for USFWS Director," https://www.dailykos.com/stories/2019/9/25/1887729/-Ties-Exposed-Between-Westlands-Water-W-D-and-Aurelia-Skipwith-Trump-s-Nominee-for-USFWS-Director.

EPILOGUE

In the preface, readers revisited a First Amendment controversy that played out in the judiciary, culminating in 2006 with the Supreme Court's decision in *Garcetti v. Ceballos*. In the face of four dissenting opinions, five justices forged a fustian (if not a Faustian) decision undermining the ability of civil servants to inform the public about key issues. In doing so, they disregarded not only the rights of federal employees but also the public's need to know in a struggling democracy.

"Need to know" about what? That's fully half the problem: We may *never* know! Might the need to know pertain to forever chemicals? The integrity of an interstate highway tunnel? The risk of accident at a nuclear facility? In a government as expansive as the U.S. version, the list would not be short. Unfortunately, for every Rachel Carson that manages to get her crucial knowledge into public discourse, we surely have John Smiths and Jane Does shut up and shut down by petty appointees and bumbling bureaucrats. Who knows how many?

Perhaps no federal career better demonstrates the price of *Garcetti v. Ceballos* than my own. Not only was my career cut to shreds by appointees and bureaucrats, but the public's need to know—in this case about the conflict between economic growth and environmental protection—was tragically underestimated and entirely disregarded. It was met instead with the politically cynical, scientifically fallacious, win-win rhetoric that "there is no conflict between growing the economy and protecting the environment."

While we can only wonder how many other civil servants have been censored and censured while pointing out the 800-pound gorilla, I have personally known roughly two dozen—in at least five agencies—who wanted to help raise public awareness about limits to growth. Not only limits to growth but the conflict between growth and crucial agency goals pertaining to environmental protection, economic sustainability, and national security. All felt stymied by agency chiefs or daunted by the challenge of swimming upstream in the river of political economy. My own experience of gag orders, reprimands, and suspensions only discouraged them further.

Readers have encountered numerous ironies in *Gag-Ordered No More*, and another has arisen in the midst of production. Gag orders—by their nature hushed affairs—are suddenly in the news; in particular the gag orders applied to the acerbic tongue of Donald Trump. As much as I have argued against gag orders in the pages above, and expressed deep frustration with the Supreme Court for its decision in *Garcetti v. Ceballos*, the courts clearly got it right with Trump. But no one should be conflating Trump's gag orders with the ones that hamstrung me. The orders against Trump are not preventing a tax-paid civil servant from communicating science-based, welfare-relevant truths to the tax-paying public. Rather, Trump's gag orders are intended to prevent his notoriously reckless, selfish polemics from endangering the health and welfare *of* civil servants doing their challenging jobs of investigation and prosecution.

Given the topic of Trump, readers should also recognize the politically non-partisan nature of *Gag-Ordered No More*, and indeed of myself as a registered Independent. After all, it's not any author's fault that Trump is a Republican (at the time of this writing, after changing his party affiliation five times). The most relevant point about Trump, given the *Gag-Ordered* context, is that no American leader has ever been more directly destructive of environmental welfare and conservation goals. As president, Trump was obsessed with GDP growth, which put him at odds with environmental protection, as demonstrated by his regulation-wrecking administration.

Yet on the topic of partisanship, or the lack thereof, it is impossible to calculate which party and which administration is ultimately more to blame for the devastation caused by a bloating GDP. A compelling case can be made that the Democratic Party, especially the Clintonian arm, has been even more damaging than Trump, albeit indirectly, by lulling the public to sleep with the win-win rhetoric that "there is no conflict between growing the economy and protecting the environment." That is the rhetoric that led me into my focus on the ecological economics of conservation, as laid out in Chapter 1, and eventually on the steady state economy as the sustainable alternative to growth.

If only an omniscient, omnipotent Truth had "gagged" (perhaps figuratively via clear thinking and clean conscience) the Clintons and their appointed ones from spewing their win-win rhetoric, the world would be a better place. Couldn't the Clintons have run instead with "It's the truth, stupid," and gone just as far with their political talents? Instead, the win-win rhetoricians cultivated by the Clintons wound up doing or directing the gagging of yours truly and other civil servants steeped in sound science and ecological economics.

Lastly, to and about the appointees and bureaucrats I gored and probably galled in *Gag-Ordered No More*: While it may have seemed like it in some pages, the book was not about you, or even about me. Rather, we each played our parts in a story that gives life to an 800-pound gorilla, which otherwise sits mummified like a seldom-seen curio at the Department of the Interior Museum. Unfortunately, like a mummy portrayed by Hollywood, its forces of destruction are at work in the world, despite its cordoned-off curation.

But, appointees and bureaucrats, Hollywood isn't knocking; the subject of economic growth seems too dry and, dug deeply into, too complicated for a pithy plot. It takes science and economics in a mix that is not for the lazy. In fact, getting any attention paid to the 800-pound gorilla—much less due diligence—is close to impossible. It takes a story, even if the story must be of strife and conflict. So you ended up playing your part, after all, in raising public awareness of the fundamental conflict between economic growth and environmental protection.

Yes, the ironies never cease.

Brian Czech
Arlington, VA
October 23, 2023

BIBLIOGRAPHY

Bacher, D. 2019. Ties Exposed Between Westlands Water W.D. and Aurelia Skipwith, Trump's Nominee for USFWS Director. *Daily Kos*, September 25. https://www.dailykos.com/stories/2019/9/25/1887729/-Ties-Exposed-Between-Westlands-Water-W-D-and-Aurelia-Skipwith-Trump-s-Nominee-for-USFWS-Director..

Bigford, T., K. Hyatt, T. Dobson, V. Poage, L. Reynolds, B. Czech, B. Hughes, J. Meldrim, P. L. Angermeier, B. Gray, J. Whitehead, L. Hushak, and F. Lupi. 2006. Economic growth and fish conservation. *Fisheries* 31(8):404-409.

Czech, B. 2021. *Supply Shock: Economic Growth at the Crossroads and the Steady State Solution.* Arlington: Steady State Press.

Czech, B. 2015. Coastal Planning on the National Wildlife Refuge System with the Sea Level Affecting Marshes Model (SLAMM). *Wetland Science and Practice* vol. 32, no. 4: 30-40.

Czech, B. 2013. Ecological economics. Pages 825-844 in N. MacLeod, editor in chief, *Grzimek's Animal Life Encyclopedia: Extinction.* Gale Cengage Learning, Detroit, Michigan.

Czech, B. 2013. The imperative of steady state economics for wild animal welfare. Pages 171-182 in M. Bekoff, ed. *Ignoring Nature No More: The Case for Compassionate Conservation.* University of Chicago Press, Chicago, Illinois.

Czech, B. 2009. Ecological economics. Pages 363-394 in *Encyclopaedia of Life Support Systems* Developed under the auspices of UNESCO-EOLSS Publishers, Oxford, UK.

Czech, B. 2009. The neoclassical production function as a relic of anti-George politics: implications for ecological economics. *Ecological Economics* 68:2193-2197.

Czech, B. 2008. Prospects for reconciling the conflict between economic growth and biodiversity conservation with technological progress. *Conservation Biology* 22(6):1389-1398.

Czech, B. 2007. The foundation of a new conservation movement: professional society positions on economic growth. *Bioscience* 57(1):6-7.

Czech, B. 2007. The steady state economy, habitat stability, and the humane treatment of wild animals. Pages 143-157 in D. Salem, ed. *The State of the Animals IV: 2007.* Humane Society Press, Washington, DC.

Czech, B. 2006. If Rome is burning, why are we fiddling? *Conservation Biology* 20(6):1563-1565.

Czech, B. 2006. Maintaining the biological integrity, diversity, and environmental health of the National Wildlife Refuge System. Pages 329-334 in D. Harmon, ed. *People, Places, and Parks.* Proceedings of the 2005 George Wright Society Conference on Parks, Protected Areas, and Cultural Sites. George Wright Society, Hancock, Michigan.

Czech, B. 2006. The steady state revolution as a prerequisite for wildlife conservation and ecological sustainability. In D. M. Lavigne, ed. *Gaining Ground: In Pursuit of Ecological Sustainability.* International Fund for Animal Welfare, Guelph, Ontario, Canada, and the University of Limerick, Limerick, Ireland.

Czech, B. 2005. The capacity of the National Wildlife Refuge System to conserve threatened and endangered animal species in the United States. *Conservation Biology* 19(4):1246-1253.

Czech, B. 2005. Urbanization as a threat to biodiversity: trophic theory, economic geography, and implications for conservation land acquisition. Pages 8-13 in D. N. Bengston, ed. *Policies for Managing Urban Growth and Landscape Change: A Key to Conservation in the 21st Century* General Technical Report NC-265. United States Department of Agriculture, Forest Service North Central Research Station, St. Paul, Minnesota.

Czech, B. 2004. A Chronological Frame of Reference for Ecological Integrity and Natural Conditions. *Natural Resources Journal* vol. 44, issue 4: 1113-1136.

Czech, B. 2004. Guest Editorial: Taking on the economic triangle! *Frontiers in Ecology and the Environment* 2(5):227.

Czech, B. 2003. Technological progress and biodiversity conservation: A dollar spent a dollar burned. *Conservation Biology* 17(5):1455-1457.

Czech, B. 2002. A transdisciplinary approach to conservation land acquisition. *Conservation Biology* 16(6):1488-1497.

Czech, B. 2002. The imperative of macroeconomics for ecologists. *Bioscience* 52(11):964-966.

Czech, B. 2002. The wildlife profession, the World Trade Center, and the conservation ethic. *Wildlife Society Bulletin* 30(1):280-281.

Czech, B. 2001. A potential catch-22 for a sustainable American ideology. *Ecological Economics* 39(1):3-12.

Czech, B. 2001. Incorporating nonhuman knowledge into the philosophy of science. *Wildlife Society Bulletin* 29(2):665-674.

Czech, B. 2000. Economic Growth as the Limiting Factor for Wildlife Conservation. *Wildlife Society Bulletin* vol. 28, no. 1: 4-14.

Czech, B. 2000. Economic growth, ecological economics, and wilderness preservation. Pages 194-200 in McCool, S. F., D. N. Cole, W. T. Borrie, and J. O'Loughlin, compilers. Wilderness Science in a Time of Change Conference, *Volume 2: Wilderness Within the Context of Larger Systems*. United States Department of Agriculture, Forest Service Proceedings RMRS-P-15-VOL-2.

Czech, B. 2000. *Shoveling Fuel for a Runaaway Train: Errant Economists, Shameful Spenders, and a Plan to Stop Them All*. Berkeley: University of California Press.

Czech, B. 2000. The importance of ecological economics to wildlife conservation. *Wildlife Society Bulletin* 28(1):2-3.

Czech, B. 1997. "The Endangered Species Act, American Democracy, and an Omnibus Role for Public Policy." PhD diss., University of Arizona, Tucson.

Czech, B. 1997. The importance of range science to federal grazing policy. *Journal of Range-Management* 50(3):326-328.

Czech, B. 1996. Challenges to establishing and implementing sound natural fire policy. *Renewable Resources Journal* 14(2):14-19.

Czech, B. 1996. Ward vs. Racehorse - Supreme Court as obviator? *Journal of the West* 35(3):61-69.

Czech, B. 1995. American Indians and wildlife conservation. *Wildlife Society Bulletin* 23(4):568-573.

Czech, B. 1995. Ecosystem management is no paradigm shift; let's try conservation. *Journal of Forestry* 93(12):17-23.

Czech, B. 1994. The feasibility of reintroducing wood bison (Bison bison athabascae) to the Yukon Flats of Alaska. Final Report to the Council of Athabascan Tribal Governments, Fort Yukon, Alaska.

Czech, B. 1993. Statement of Brian Czech (Director, San Carlos Recreation and Wildlife Department, San Carlos Apache Tribe). Pages 183-189 in Report of the Oversight Hearing before the Committee on Natural Resources, House of Representatives, One Hundred Third Congress. U.S. Government Printing Office, Serial No. 103-5.

Czech, B., S. K. Alam, P. A. Angermeier, S. M. Coghlan, G. F. Hartman, L. Krall, J. V. Mead, T. G. Northcote, P. Pister, K. M. Reed, C. A. Rose, J. A. Thompson, and P. F. Thompson. 2006. Economic growth, fish conservation, and the American Fisheries Society: conclusion to a forum, beginning of a movement? *Fisheries* 31(1):40-43.

Czech, B., E. Allen, D. Batker, P. Beier, H. Daly, J. Erickson, P. Garrettson, V. Geist, J. Gowdy, L. Greenwalt, H. Hands, P. Krausman, P. Magee, C. Miller, K. Novak, G. Pullis, C. Robinson, J. Santa-Barbara, J. Teer, D. Trauger, and C. Willer. 2003. The iron triangle: Why The Wildlife Society needs to take a position on economic growth. *Wildlife Society Bulletin* 31(2):574-577.

Czech, B., P. Angermeier, H. Daly, P. Pister, and R. Hughes. 2004. Fish conservation, sustainable fisheries, and economic growth: No more fish stories. *Fisheries* 29(8):36-37.

Czech, B., and R. Borkhataria. 2001. The Relationship of Political Party Affiliation to Wildlife Conservation Attitudes. *Politics and the Life Sciences* vol. 20, no. 1: 3-12.

Czech, B., S. Covington, T.M. Crimmins, J.A. Ericson, C. Flather, M. Gale, K. Gerst, M. Higgins, M. Kaib, E. Marino, T. Moran, J. Morton, Neal Niemuth, H. Peckett, D. Savignano, L. Saperstein, S. Skorupa, E. Wagener, B. Wilen, and B. Wolfe. 2014. *Planning for climate change on the National Wildlife Refuge System*. U.S. Fish and Wildlife Service, National Wildlife Refuge System, Washington, DC. 132pp.

Czech, B., and H. Daly. 2004. The steady state economy: what it is, entails, and connotes. *Wildlife Society Bulletin* 32(2):598-605.

Czech, B., P. K. Devers, and P. R. Krausman. 2001. The relationship of gender to species conservation attitudes. *Wildlife Society Bulletin* 29(1):187-194.

Czech, B., R. Heitschmidt, J. Brown, and A. Hild 2008. Sustainable rangeland management, economic growth, and a cautious role for the SRM. *Rangelands* 30(6):33-37.

Czech, B., and P. R. Krausman. 2001. *The Endangered Species Act: History, Conservation Biology, and Public Policy*. Baltimore: Johns Hopkins University Press.

Czech, B., and P. R. Krausman. 1999. Controversial wildlife management issues in southwestern U.S. wilderness. *International Journal of Wilderness* 5(3):22-28.

Czech, B., and P. R. Krausman. 1999. Public Opinion on Endangered Species Conservation and Policy. *Society and Natural Resources* vol. 12 issue 5: 469-479.

Czech, B., and P. R. Krausman. 1998. The species concept, species prioritization, and the technical legitimacy of the Endangered Species Act. *Transactions of the North American Wildlife and Natural Resources Conference* 62:514-524.

Czech, B., and P. R. Krausman. 1997. Distribution and Causation of Species Endangerment in the United States. *Science* vol. 277 issue 5329: 1116-1117.

Czech, B., and P. R. Krausman. 1997. Implications of an ecosystem management literature review. *Wildlife Society Bulletin* 25(3):667-675.

Czech, B., and P. R. Krausman. 1997. Public opinion on species and endangered species conservation. *Endangered Species Update* 14(5&6):7-10.

Czech, B., P. R. Krausman, and R. Borkhataria. 1998. Social construction, political power, and the allocation of benefits to endangered species. *Conservation Biology* 12:1103-1112.

Czech, B., P. R. Krausman, and P. K. Devers. 2000. Economic Associations among Causes of Species Endangerment in the United States. *BioScience* vol. 50, no. 7: 593-601.

Czech, B., J. H. Mills Busa, and R. M. Brown. 2012. Effects of economic growth on biodiversity in the United States. *Natural Resources Forum* 36:160-166.

Czech, B., K. Murphy, S. Berendzen, D. Blankinship, B. Byrd, S. Gard, D. Kuzmeskus, H. Laskowski, J. Mattson, S. Van Riper, T. Zimmerman. 2002. A process for integrating wildlife population, biodiversity, and habitat goals and objectives on the National Wildlife Refuge System: coordinating with partners at all landscape scales. U.S. Fish and Wildlife Service, Washington, D.C.

Czech, B., and P. Pister. 2005. Economic growth, fish conservation, and the American Fisheries Society: Introduction to a special series. *Fisheries* 30(1):38-40.

Czech, B., P. Pister, and L. Krall. 2005. A special class of neoclassical economists. *Fisheries* 30(4):34-35.

Czech, B., and R. B. Richardson. 2011. The economics of cumulative effects: ecological and macro by nature. Pages 63-80 in P. R. Krausman and L. K. Harris, eds. *Cumulative Effects in Wildlife Management: A Critical Aspect of Impact Mitigation*. Taylor and Francis, London.

Daly, H. E., B. Czech, D. L. Trauger, W. E. Rees, M. Grover, T. Dobson, and S. C. Trombulak. 2007. Are we consuming too much – for what? *Conservation Biology* 21:1359-1362.

Daly, H. E., and J. Farley. 2010. *Ecological Economics: Principles and Applications*. Washington, DC: Island Press.

Dietz, R., and B. Czech. 2005. Conservation deficits for the continental United States: an ecosystem gap analysis. *Conservation Biology* 19(5):1478-1487.

Dresner, S. 2002. *The Principles of Sustainability*. London: Earthscan.

Fischman, R. L. 2003. *The National Wildlife Refuges: Coordinating a Conservation System Through Law*. Washington, DC: Island Press.

Fischman, R. L. 2002. The National Wildlife Refuge System and the Hallmarks of Modern Organic Legislation. *Ecology Law Quarterly* vol. 29: 457-622.

Fischman, R, and R. Adamcik. 2011. Beyond trust species: the conservation potential of the National Wildlife Refuge System in the wake of climate change. *Natural Resources Journal* vol. 51: 1-33.

Gates, E., D. Trauger, and B. Czech, eds. 2014. *Peak Oil, Economic Growth, and Wildlife Conservation*. Springer, New York. 346pp.

General Services Administration. 2009. "The New Sustainable Frontier: Principles of Sustainable Development." GSA Office of Governmentwide Policy, Washington, DC.

Gowdy, J., C. Hall, K. Klitgaard, and L. Krall. 2010. What every conservation biologist should know about economic theory. *Conservation Biology* vol. 24, no. 6: 1440-1447.

Hamilton, S. F., T. D. Lustig, T. C. Roberts, Jr., S. W. Albrecht, J. Campbell, K. E. Nelson, B. Czech, and K. Kuhlman. 2004. Indicators of legal, institutional, and economic framework for rangeland conservation and sustainable management. *Journal of Range Management.*

Huettmann, F., and B. Czech. 2006. The steady state economy for global shorebird and habitat conservation. *Endangered Species Research* 2:89-92

Mayer, J. *Dark Money: The Hidden History of the Billionaires Behind the Rise of the Radical Right.* 2017. New York: Doubleday.

McCorkle, R. 2018. "Conflict of Interest at the U.S. Fish and Wildlife Service? A Deal Some Couldn't Refuse." *The Daly News,* March 20, https: //steadystate.org/ conflict-of-interest-at-the-u-s-fish-and-wildlife-service-and-divesting-from-fossil-fuel/.

McNeill, J. R. 2000. *Something New under the Sun: An Environmental History of the Twentieth-Century World.* New York: W.W. Norton.

Miller-Reed, K., and B. Czech. 2005. Causes of fish endangerment in the United States, or the structure of the American economy. *Fisheries* 30(7):36-38.

Pergams, O. R. W., B. Czech, J. C. Haney, and D. Nyberg. 2004. Linkage of conservation activity to trends in the U.S. economy. *Conservation Biology* 18(6):1617-1623.

Ruane, K. A. 2014. "Freedom of speech and press: exceptions to the First Amendment." Washington, DC Congressional Research Service.

Speth, J. G. 2022. *They Knew. The US Federal Government's Fifty-Year Role in Causing the Climate Crisis.* Cambridge, MA: MIT Press.

Tear, T. H., P. Karieva, P. L. Angermeir, P. Comer, B. Czech, R. Kautz, L. Landon, D. Mehlman, K. Murphy, M. Ruckelshaus, J. M. Scott, and G. Wilhere. 2005. How much is enough? The recurrent problem of setting measurable objectives in conservation. *Bioscience* 55:835-849.

The Wildlife Society. 2003. "The relationship of economic growth to wildlife conservation." *The Wildlife Society: Technical Review* 03-1.

Tuan, Yi-Fu. 1977. *Space and Place: The Perspective of Experience.* Minneapolis: University of Minnesota Press.

Udall Center. 1998. *Digest of the pygmy-owl forum.* The Udall Center for Studies in Public Policy, University of Arizona, Tucson.

USDA. 2004. "National Report on Sustainable Forests - 2003." FS-766, U.S. Department of Agriculture, Forest Service, Washington, DC.

U.S. Fish and Wildlife Service. 2001. Policy on maintaining the biological integrity, diversity, and environmental health of the National Wildlife Refuge System. *Federal Register* 66(10):3810-3823.

U.S. Fish and Wildlife Service. 2000. Draft policy on maintaining the ecological integrity of the National Wildlife Refuge System. *Federal Register* 66(10):61356-61362.

INDEX

800-pound gorilla (including instances of "800-Pound Gorilla"), 5, 12, 16–17, 31, 34–35, 37–39, 41, 45–46, 51–53, 56, 59, 63, 67, 69–73, 75, 78, 80, 82–83, 85, 88–97, 101–103, 109–111, 116–117

A

Africa, 105, 109
Alabama, 92, 94, 96, 124
Alaska National Interest Lands Conservation Act, 79
Alaska, 28, 40, 43, 45, 55, 64, 73, 79, 103–104, 108–109, 117, 124
Alberres, Erin, 18–19, 86
American Civil Liberties Union (ACLU), 52
American Economic Association, 47
American Fisheries Society, 18, 54, 74, 77, 95
Anchorage, Alaska, 104, 113
Angermeier, Paul, 37
Apaches, 9
Arctic National Wildlife Refuge, 79

B

Bayou Farewell, 89
Bean, Michael, 83
Beer, 8, 16, 55, 65, 78, 80, 108–109, 111
Benson, Arizona, 7
Bentley, Robert, 94
Bible Club, 8, 51, 53, 55, 60, 65, 72–74, 78–80, 83, 86, 88–89, 97, 102, 105–106, 108–111, 116–117
Biden Administration, 112
"Big Six" priority uses (of national wildlife refuges), 61
Biodiversity (see also "biological diversity"), 5–6, 15–16, 21, 32–34, 52, 61–63, 68, 76, 90–95, 101, 115–116, 123, 127–128
Biological diversity (see also "biodiversity"), 4, 13–15
Biological integrity (see "ecological integrity")

Bison, 38–40, 121
Bold Ideas Forum, 59–74, 76–79, 81, 96
Buenos Aires National Wildlife Refuge, 40
Bureau of Indian Affairs (BIA), 10
Bureau of Land Management (BLM), 12, 61, 125
Bush, President George W., 26, 86, 90, 103, 124

C

Cahaba River National Wildlife Refuge, 94
Cahoon, Don, 87
"Carter Incident", 78–79, 81–82, 88
Carson, Rachel, 67, 102, 131
Carter, President Jimmy, 32, 78–82, 88, 97
Caterpillar, 11, 18
Center for the Advancement of the Steady State Economy (CASSE), 53-55, 66–67, 77, 93, 95–97, 102, 107, 116
China, 109, 111
Chronological frame of reference (for natural conditions), 39–42, 126
Clark, Jamie, 22, 25–28, 41, 46–47, 53, 67
Climate change, 8, 10, 19, 31, 40, 55, 63, 82–86, 88–90, 93, 101, 109, 111, 115, 121, 127–128
Clinton Administration, 16
Clinton, Bill, 16
Coarse filter (for biodiversity conservation; see also "Ecosystem conservation"), 62–64
Coast Range Association, 74
Coleman, Rick, 20–22, 27–28, 53, 65, 67
Common sense, 7, 20, 34, 39, 118
Compatible use (of national wildlife refuges), 61, 127
Congress, U.S., 3, 10, 18, 24, 119, 124, 127, 129
Conservation biology, 10, 13–16, 18, 20–21, 44, 54, 62–64, 77, 93, 95, 116, 127
Conservation ethic, 19–20, 104, 112, 123, 128–129
Conservation return on investment, 19
Conserving the Future, 60, 65, 72, 96, 127
COP21, 108–109

Corruption, 72, 76, 101–102
Council of Athabascan Tribal Governments, 40
Council of Economic Advisors, 32, 67, 69
COVID, 129
Crab Orchard National Wildlife Refuge, 126
Crasche, Dan, 21–22, 28, 34, 47, 51–52, 57, 59–60, 64-67, 71–74, 80, 82, 89, 95, 97, 102, 111

D
Dallas, Texas, 8
Daly, Herman, 28, 56
Defenders of Wildlife, 27
Democracy, 21, 23, 57, 65, 70
Denver, Colorado, 55, 106, 113
Desert National Wildlife Refuge, 124
Diamond, Jared, 56
DIDS (Dumb-It-Down Syndrome), 115–120
Dietz, Rob, 54, 66–67, 96
Dirth, Tim, 44-47, 51-55, 57, 59–60, 65, 74, 77–78, 80–81, 83, 89, 92, 95, 97, 102, 109–111
Division of Fisheries and Habitat Conservation (of the Fish and Wildlife Service), 104
Division of Natural Resources and Conservation Planning (at National Wildlife Refuge System headquarters), 66, 75, 78, 110

E
Earth Day, 67, 69, 72, 74
Earth Economics, 74
Earth Summit (1992), 90
Ecological economics, 18, 21–22, 24, 27, 53–55, 66–68, 76, 83, 102, 110, 116, 122
Ecological integrity policy, 37–38, 41, 43–44, 62, 91, 125–126
Ecological integrity, 37–46, 61–62, 73, 91–93, 121, 123, 125–126, 128, 130
Ecological macroeconomics, 16–18, 42, 67–69, 93, 95, 122, 129
Ecological Services Program (of the Fish and Wildlife Service), 54, 104

Ecological Society of America, 18, 54, 77, 95
Economic growth, 5–6, 8–9, 12, 16–18, 21–25, 27, 29-35, 39, 42–43, 46–47, 51–55, 67–69, 71–74, 77, 79, 85, 90–91, 95–97, 101–103, 110–111, 116, 121–123, 125, 128–129
Ecosystem conservation (see also "Coarse filter"), 63–65, 120 66, 68
Elk, 9–10
Endangered Species Act, 4–5, 11–12, 18–19, 24, 33, 61, 67, 77, 79, 83, 119, 123, 126,
Environmental health, 37–38, 44, 46
Environmental Protection Agency (EPA), 30, 32–33, 53, 112

F
Federal Geographic Data Committee, 64
Federal Reserve, 23, 32
Fishing, 8, 13-15, 24, 61, 92–93, 108, 122, 125–127
Florida, 19, 64, 86, 109, 120
Fox, Jimmy, 69, 73
Freedom of Information Act (FOIA), 19, 107–108
Friends of the Earth, 74
Fulfilling the Promise, 60, 65, 127
Full Employment and Balanced Growth Act of 1978, 124

G
Gag-order creep, 51–57
GDP (gross domestic product), 23, 29–33, 63, 68, 83–84, 103, 124–125, 127
General Services Administration, 69, 103
Geronimo, 9
Giffords, Gabby, 3
Glyphosate (aka Roundup, as opposed to the "glyphosphate" of Dick Schultz notoriety), 8
Goodall, Jane, 77, 124, 130
Government Accountability Office, 52, 69
"Green growth," 124, 127–128
Greenhouse gas emissions, 31, 83
Greenwalt, Lynn, 54, 56, 67, 77, 124, 130
Grizzly bear(s), 11, 103, 108, 118
Guldin, Rich, 91
Gulf of Mexico Alliance, 87
Gulf of Mexico, 64, 86, 89, 92

Guntensbergen, Glen, 87

H
Haaland, Deb, 112
Harvard, 93-94, 96
Haufler, Jonathan, 17-18
Herz, Jonathan, 74
Hiring practices, 128-129
Homer, Alaska, 108
Honolulu, 104, 113
Hook-and-bullet wildlife management, 8, 14-15, 21
Houston, TX, 89
Hunting, 8-9, 13-15, 41, 61, 73, 92-93, 106, 121-122, 126-127
Hurricane Harvey, 85
Hurricane Irene, 85
Hurricane Sandy, 85

I
Ingram, Helen, 11
Inspector General, 52, 120
Institutional reform, 128-130
Intergovernmental Panel on Climate Change, 84, 127
International Society for Ecological Economics, 18
Invasive species, 15, 62-63, 68

K
Karr, James, 37
Koch Brothers, 55
Kodiak Island, 103-105, 108
Kolbe, Jim, 3-4
Krausman, Paul, 11

L
Land Acquisition Priority System (LAPS), 19, 97, 117, 119-120
Land acquisition, 19, 82, 86-87, 92-93, 101, 116-117, 119-120
Land and Water Conservation Fund, 19, 120
Landscape(s), 10, 13, 15, 41, 43-44, 61, 63, 68
Leopold, Aldo, 15, 24, 78, 123
Lewis and Clark, 41
Little Ice Age, 40
Lombardi, Vince, 126

Lyze, Arun, 56-57, 59, 88-89, 102, 105-106

M
Madison, Wisconsin, 67, 71, 97
Mallards, 62-63
Martinis, Cynthia, 105-106, 108
McDaniel, Carl, 47
McNeil, J.R., 42
Medieval Warm Period, 40
Mercatus Center, 26
Merit Service Protection Board, 81
Microeconomics, 15, 69
Mobile-Tensaw Delta, 92-94, 96-97
Montreal Process, 90
Murie, Olaus, 67, 102

N
National Conservation Training Center (NCTC), 16, 79, 103, 124, 128
National Council for Science and the Environment, 28, 95
National Environmental Policy Act (NEPA), 101
National Geographic, 103
National Goals Team, 62, 64
National Oceanic and Atmospheric Administration, 89
National Report on Sustainable Forests, 90
National Research Council, 52, 54
National Science Foundation, 51, 54
National security, 23, 32, 34
National Vegetation Classification System, 63
National Wetlands Inventory, 8, 87, 104
National Wildlife Federation, 47
National Wildlife Refuge System Improvement Act of 1997, 13, 37-39, 43-44, 60-62, 125, 127
National Wildlife Refuge System, 13-14, 16, 18-22, 27, 34, 37-39, 43-45, 47, 51-55, 60-68, 72-73, 76, 79, 83, 85-91, 93, 95-97, 101-110, 112-113, 116-117, 119-120, 124-126
Native Americans, 41-42
Natural conditions, 37-39, 41-42, 125-126
Natural Heritage programs, 64
(The) Nature Conservancy (TNC), 19, 51, 64
New Orleans, Louisiana, 104-105

New York City, 41
North American Wildlife and Natural Resources Conference, 119

O
Obama Administration, 113
Obama, President Barack, 115
Office of Special Counsel, 52
Owl, cactus ferruginous pygmy, 4, 12

P
Pacific Northwest, 4, 8, 28
Panther, Florida, 121
Paris, 108-109, 111
Paris Climate Accords (see also "COP21"), 108
Patterson, Neil, 93
Per-diem bonus, 76, 97, 105–106
Peter Principle, 53
Phoenix, Arizona, 8
Plain Writing Act of 2010, 115
Planning for Climate Change on the National Wildlife Refuge System, 83–84, 88
Planning, 20, 63–64, 83–84, 86–89, 93–94, 96, 109, 116
Pock, Debra, 59, 77–83, 102, 116–117
Pruitt, Scott, 112
Public Employees for Environmental Responsibility (PEER), 19, 78
Pudert, Geoff, 59, 75–77, 81, 83, 89, 102, 105–106

R
Radloff, David, 91
Rangeland Health, 91
Rees, William, 56
Region 4 (of the U.S. Fish and Wildlife Service), 94, 96
Rennselaer Polytechnic Institute, 47
Rey, Mark, 90
Roosevelt, Theodore, 60, 113
Rostow, W.W., 42
Roundtable on Sustainable Forests, 90–91
Roundtable on Sustainable Rangelands, 91

Ruyle, George, 91

S
Sack, Jay, 80
San Carlos Apache Reservation, 7, 9, 37
San Francisco Bay National Wildlife Refuge, 21
Sand County Almanac, 15
Schultz, Dick, 7–8, 59, 86
Schumacher, E.F., 79
Sea Level Affecting Marshes Model (SLAMM), 86–89, 109
Sea-level rise, 8, 19, 85–90, 92–93, 109, 120
Seattle, Washington, 8, 104
Seaze, Chris, 45, 59
Secretary of the Interior, 29, 31, 33–34, 37, 112, 125
Selbo, Sarena, 83–84, 88
Shelby, Senator Richard, 94
Shepherdstown, West Virginia, 16, 79
Shoveling Fuel for a Runaway Train, 12, 17, 53–54
Siekaniec, Greg, 34
Silent Spring, 102
Slayem, Ryan, 108
Smerfeld, John, 109–111
Society for Conservation Biology, 15, 18, 54, 77, 95
Society of Environmental Journalists, 53
Souheaver, Elizabeth, 46-47, 59
Speth, Gus, 90
Spotted owl, Mexican, 10
Spotted owl, northern, 4
Steady state economy, 6, 12, 16, 22, 24, 32–34, 53–54, 56–57, 78, 112, 124, 127–128
Steady-state economics, 28, 123–124, 128, 130
Supply Shock, 55–56
Supreme Court, 10
Surrogate species approach (to conservation), 64–65
Sustainability, 23, 32, 34, 69, 73–74, 79, 90–91
Sustainable development
Sustainable Water Roundtable, 91

Suzuki, David, 77

T
Taxpayers, 4, 8, 16, 19, 22, 39, 64-65, 75, 89, 97, 101, 104–105, 107–109, 111, 113, 115, 120, 122
Temple, Stanley, 14
Texas, 86, 89, 115
The Wildlife Society, 17–18, 54, 69, 74, 77, 130
Tiglax (research vessel), 108
Toomey, Officer Keith, 81
True Conservation, 121–130
Trump Administration, 112, 129
Trump, Donald, 103, 112–113, 124, 130, 1311-132
Trust species, 21, 39, 63, 72
Trust, Kim, 83
Tuan, Yi-Fu, 46
Tucson, 3-4, 6, 21

U
U.S. Department of the Interior, 10, 13–14, 18, 33, 75, 101, 123, 130
U.S. Forest Service, 12, 53, 61, 90–91
U.S. Geological Survey (USGS), 26, 64, 87, 89
U.S. Park Service, 12, 38, 53, 61
U.S. Society for Ecological Economics, 18, 24, 68, 74, 130
University of Arizona, 4, 7, 11, 17, 116

V
Virginia Tech, 66, 93

W
Washington, DC, 5, 7, 10, 12, 16, 28, 51, 53, 81, 93, 95, 103–104, 110
Waste, fraud, and abuse, 19, 120
Watercress Darter National Wildlife Refuge, 124
Wayburn, Thomas, 74
White House, 16, 29, 79, 110
Wildlife first principle, 60-61
Wilen, Bill, 8
Williams, Martha, 126
Wilson, E.O., 14, 77, 92–97, 124, 130

Win-win rhetoric, 21-23, 27, 47, 74, 95, 102, 123, 127
Wisconsin, 7–8, 14, 67, 115–116
Wolves, 38–39, 73, 119

Y
Young, Don, 43, 45
Yukon Flats, 40

Z
Zinke, Ryan, 112

www.ingramcontent.com/pod-product-compliance
Lightning Source LLC
Chambersburg PA
CBHW052143070526
44585CB00017B/1947